The Simple Secrets of

CROWDFUNDING

Using the Internet to Fund... Everything

By Michael S. Melfi

ABOUT THE AUTHOR

 Michael S. Melfi is an Intellectual Property attorney and entrepreneur. Michael has a dynamic background that allows him to provide insightful legal services, while creating business development strategies. Michael is focused on creating value for his clients through a portfolio of products including programming and training to develop successful entrepreneurs.

Over the last decade Michael founded and led a national multi-media company. As COO & General Counsel Michael pioneered various experiential and digital marketing campaigns for Fortune 500 clients. As a thought leader and innovator, Michael utilized digital marketing and various Social Media platforms to develop an online presence for his company in the top 1% of all websites globally. Through these experiences and involvement with the digital platform, Michael gained valuable insight into the legal and business ramifications of the Internet and including Social Media.

Michael understands entrepreneurs, because he is one. Part of being an entrepreneur is seeing an opportunity and moving through uncertainty to take advantage of those situations, as well as understanding how to deal with the obstacles. His work with entrepreneurial companies has helped him understand how to create an Identity of being a successful entrepreneur.

By developing this identity, an entrepreneur can create success around an idea, or business - without this shift in identity growth becomes impossible.

CONTENTS

INTRODUCTION

WELCOME

The purpose of this book is to provide an inside track on an industry that is still in it's infancy, a new financial model that is currently redefining the small business landscape, and its foundation lies in the conscious business principle of crowdsourcing. If you have not heard of it, we will introduce you to the concept of crowdfunding. If you are familiar with crowdfunding, we will to go into the details of what it is, why it is so valuable, and how to take part in one of the fastest growing markets. You most likely have picked this book because you are curious to know more about crowdfunding, have a campaign going, or just want to understand what everyone else is talking about. No matter what your personal interest in crowdfunding is, we are confident this book will offer you additional insight.

Since some say the industry is still the 'Wild Wild West,' in this book we attempt to create some clarity through gathering the best of all the information that is currently available for consumption, and create a simple roadmap for you to follow. The style of this book is to present the information in such a way that it is easy to understand so that you can get something valuable out of the content. Additionally, in the second half of the book we will be providing various strategies and tactics to manage a successful project that we hope you will find insightful and very beneficial.

We know that there will be varying degrees of understanding of crowdfunding, and you will be opening this book from a variety of perspectives. Perhaps you've heard the names Kickstarter or Indiegogo, maybe you clicked on a friend's Facebook post and donated a few dollars to a charitable cause. On the other side, maybe you have a developed business idea and want ideas on how to get funded, with no idea where to start. Or maybe you have launched a project on a portal, and it may or may not have succeeded. No matter where you're at, this book can help teach you what crowdfunding is, why it's valuable and go beyond into the makings of a successful campaign.

Crowdfunding At A Glance

What is Crowdfunding?

Crowdfunding is the process of asking the general public for contributions to fund a new project. This project could be a business, charity or artistic venture. Crowdfunding is innovative because it allows entrepreneurs to bypass the "middleman" (i.e. venture capitalists, grants, or other funding sources) and connect directly with consumers who are genuinely interested in making the creator's vision a reality. The project owners are the ones who "create" the presentation on a portal, which is a website on the Internet. Project owners connect with the audience (crowd) and shares their idea with prospective supporters. The hope is to capture the interest, and spur action of a certain group in the crowd, who then choose to contribute to, or fund the campaign. This makes them "funders." The transaction is hosted and processed by a

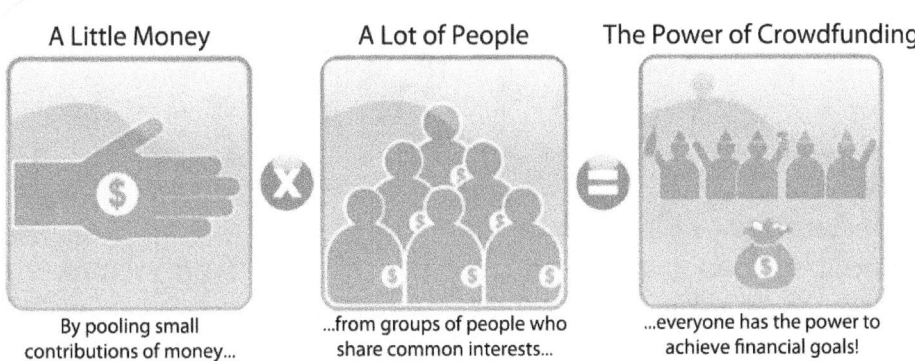

A Little Money	A Lot of People	The Power of Crowdfunding
By pooling small contributions of money...	...from groups of people who share common interests...	...everyone has the power to achieve financial goals!

Crowdfunding "portal" or "platform."
Crowdfunding is all about sharing wealth and ideas in ways that were less effective and efficient prior to the advent of the Internet. Crowdfunding helps to create products and markets that might have never been born!

When analyzing the Crowdfunding model, there are advantages and disadvantages:

Advantages to the CF Model

- Forge early and strong relationships with customers; these become your marketing team

- Continuous, transparent conversation with consumers

- There's room for more potential investors since you can solicit the general public

- The crowd allows you to pitch to any- and everyone; test validity of new concepts; little startup cost

- Easy to monitor and manage - from your own kitchen table!

- Don't always give away equity

- Control of the fundraising for the business or project

Disadvantages to Model

- Difficult/stressful (you are doing everything, and are completely accountable for your success or failure)

- Lots of preparation beyond normal product pitches (need actual evidence of potential beyond proof of concept)

- Idea could be stolen (out in the public, no way to operate on stealth)

- It never ends; need ongoing social marketing campaigns/self-promotion

- Have to be very creative about drumming up interest in your project

- Doesn't always work. Let's be honest; some ideas just aren't a good fit for CF

- Varied (and sometimes conflicting) expectations/demands from diverse group of funders
- Competition: against other interesting projects, with the same audience with their same amount of disposable income.

As you read this introduction, you may have asked yourself: Why crowdfunding, why now? There are a few reasons to subscribe to this seemingly recent phenomena according to some thought leaders in the industry.

First, there are a few key sites that have gained a lot of momentum and have made the concept very popular. These sites have paved the way and created awareness for the general public, laying the foundation for the industry to grow. Examples are Kickstarter, Indiegogo and Crowdrise.

Secondly, and more importantly, crowdfunding success is based on the ability of your project's message to get amplified by the crowd. As the Internet has become a Web 2.0 environment and Social Media has infiltrated our daily lives, the ability for a project to share a message with family and friends, who will then share with their family and friends, creates the amplification necessary to achieve the needed success.

Thirdly, the JOBS Act (discussed in-depth in the "Back Home" section in Chapter One) has made the limit on the number of shareholders for a given company much bigger, and public seeking of investors legal. Finally, the concept of raising funds is a relatively old concept and many organizations such as the Red Cross or March of Dimes have been successfully raising funds online for many years.

The difference is that the fundraiser has gone from being an organization, association or group, to individuals, thought leaders and passionate supporters.

We invite you to read this book all the way through, hunt and peck, or simply keep as a definitive guide to crowdfunding. No matter your approach to learning about crowdfunding, there's something in this for you.

HISTORY
In the Beginning

Long before Kickstarter, Indiegogo, Veronica Mars, and shiny gadgets, crowdfunding began taking root in the minds of businessmen. The first instance similar to crowdfunding seen today came in the form of praenumeration, a type of subscription from the 18th century in Germany.

In this model, the publisher offered a to-be-written book to groups at a discount, allowing him to cover costs in advance. Throughout history, magazines also used this model to forecast the number of subscribers accurately.

In the same century, popular writer Jonathan Swift started one of the more popular micro lending programs, the Irish Loan Fund. This fund was designed to give loans to low-income families in rural areas. By the 1800s, the program was at its peak, with twenty percent of all households participating in it. Some 300 other programs like this had also started, proving it to be a valuable model for loans.

Towards the end of the 19th century, across the pond, Lady Liberty was in danger of not being displayed. In 1887, the American Committee for the Statue of Liberty ran out of money to fund the statue's pedestal. Newspaper publisher Joseph Pulitzer urged the citizens of New York city to donate towards this pedestal through his newspaper, the New York World. Pulitzer pledged to print the name of every contributor, no matter how small the amount given. The drive captured the imagination of New Yorkers, especially when Pulitzer began publishing the notes he received from contributors. With donations from children as low as 5 cents, the diversity of groups involved was inspiring.

As the donations flooded in, the committee resumed work on the pedestal. In June, 1885 New Yorkers displayed their new-found enthusiasm for the statue, as the French vessel Isère arrived with the crates holding the disassembled statue on board. Two hundred thousand people lined the docks and hundreds of boats put to sea to welcome the Isère. After five months of daily calls to donate to the statue fund, on August 11, 1885, the World announced that $102,000 had been raised from 120,000 donors, and that 80 percent of the total had been received in sums of less than one dollar. Lady Liberty was saved. This resembles some of the most successful campaigns today, timing, collection point, and monies considered. It remains one of Pulitzer's proudest achievements.

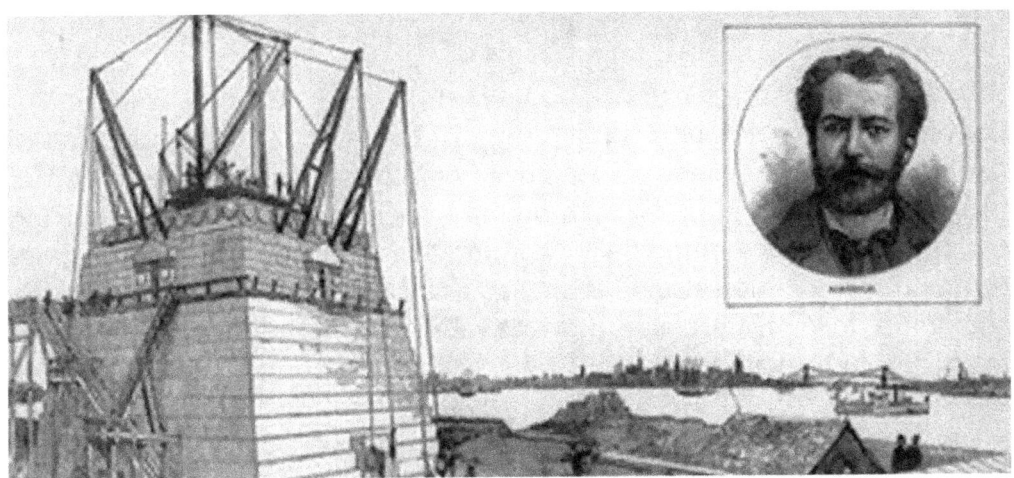

Fast forwarding a bit, we see the closest form of CF today to be microlending, or microfinance. Dr. Muhammad Yunus has often been credited as a pioneer for microfinance. In 1976, he began a research project with his graduate students in Bangladesh. His goal with the project was to create self-employment opportunities for the poor, banking opportunities for the low-income, and to eliminate exploitation of the poor. This would happen through a series of small loans for a short time, which he discovered could make a huge difference to a person of this economic status.

The first round was to 42 women in a village that specialized in bamboo production. Before Yunus, these women had to take out usurious loans to pay for basic production costs. He believed that the poor would repay, given the chance. Loaning $27 to each woman, this process became a success. Soon after, he secured a loan from the government that allowed him to give more small loans to the poor. Within 5 years, the program boasted 30,000 members, and in 1983, became Greeman Bank. Today, the bank has 8 million borrowers, with 97% of the money going towards businesses operated by women. In 2006, the bank was awarded the Nobel Peace Prize for social and economic development.

As you can see by these examples, Crowdfunding has been in play long before now and its uses have evolved from helping fund the Statue of Liberty pedestal to helping fund the economy of the poor, to helping fund all types of projects. Crowdfunding is not the only use of the crowd; another evolution of Crowdfunding is Crowdsourcing, a different way to get and stay involved.

The Early Days of "Crowdfunding"

What is Crowdsourcing?

Crowdsourcing, a more general term, is the act of outsourcing tasks, traditionally performed by an employee or contractor, to a large group of people or community (a crowd), through an open invite (call). Crowdsourcing is typically enabled through online communities consisting of members with common skills or interests and is applied as a model that enables individuals and groups to innovate, create, produce, report, predict, collaborate, fund and to engage customers.

In the words of Crowdsourcing.org, crowdsourcing is the place you go "...if you want to join the debate!" Essentially, crowdsourcing is based off the "wisdom of crowds" premise - a group of people constantly improving or commenting on something will create the best possible product. The website crowdsourcing. org is a place to connect with industry experts, share content and ideas, and promote any ventures you have created. People use it for a variety of reasons, mainly to get connected to other like-minded business people. Learn, Share, Connect, these are the key words on the value-add of the website.

"Crowdsourcing works because you're leveraging many ideas instead of one. This usually leads to a better outcome."

Patrick Llewyllen
CEO of 99Designs

According to Patrick Llewyllen, CEO of 99Designs, "crowdsourcing works because you're leveraging many ideas instead of one. This usually leads to a better outcome."

99Designs is a company that allows one company to post a brief about a logo needed in the form of a "contest," then other designers "compete" to create the best one.

Then the company chooses their favorite logo, and the copyright agreement is signed. This wildly successful form of crowdsourcing came about in Australia, and according to Llewyllen, was really just meant to be something for fun on the forum of PsiPoint.com - an educational site for designers. Very quickly, this forum exploded with briefs and contests, and the concept evolved into a valuable business model, begetting 99Designs.

CASE STUDY:
CROWDSOURCING IN ACTION: POCKET TRIPOD

Picked up in articles by Gizmodo and Mashable, two tech, news, and entertainment blogs, the Kickstarter for the Pocket Tripod was an immediate success. One of the things the Tripod team needed, however, were eye-catchingly designed t-shirts as rewards for their backers. Briefing the designing community on 99Designs.com, they were able to come up with both a logo and an amazing tshirt design, befitting of the brand.

This is a classic example of crowdsourcing. The prompt was simple enough: for designers to get to know their brand and come up with a great design for a t-shirt that would engage potential users. Using 99Designs, Pocket Tripod was able to have its pick from several designers on an easy-to-use Internet interface, rather than going the traditional route of hiring a design team.

In the late 1990's Internet communities began to exchange content, and get rallied behind a series of causes (charitable idea discussion, artist/musician fandom, etc.). The British rock band Marillion used the Internet to fund a national tour in 1997. They raised $60,000 in donations from their fans through their website. The idea was actually conceived by a band advocate, but Marillion used the same technique to fund subsequent albums over the next decade.

Along the same idea, the first actual crowdfunding platform came in 2000. The creators dubbed it "ArtistShare," and used it as a space for fans to fund the albums, etc. of their favorite musicians. Work on this pioneering platform has received 6 Grammy Awards and several nominations.*Other reward-based crowdfunding platforms, such as Sellaband (2006), Indiegogo (2008), and Kickstarter (2009) followed.
*http://artistshare.com/v4/About

By 2011, crowdfunding on a platform such as Kickstarter or Indiegogo was thought to be reserved for starving artists and entrepreneurial misfits. Indiegogo was the first to appear, officially launching at the Sundance Film Festival. Creator Danae Ringelmann, a theater director, wanted to seek alternative revenue streams by working on indie films. He created a platform to get these and other more artistic-focused projects funded. Over time, these projects gained more and more popularity, soon being perceived as "legitimate" by all eyes on the project.

Kickstarter is a funding platform for creative projects such as films, games, music, art, design, and technology. It was launched in April, 2009 and was previously known as KickStartr. It is now considered to be the most successful crowdfunding sites in the U.S. Since its inception Kickstarter has launched over 76,000 projects and collected approximately $350 million, pledged by more than 2.5 million people. We discuss Kickstarter a great deal in this book because it has been such a key player in generating mainstream interest and understanding of the crowdfunding model.

Kickstarter employs an all-or-nothing funding policy. This strategy has resulted in:

- Successful funded projects of 44%.

- 12% of projects finished without having ever received a single pledge, or contribution towards the campaign.

- 82% of projects that raised more than 20% of their goal were successfully funded. According to Kickstarter's CEO, the company has no plans to enter into Equity-based Crowdfunding.

Their publicity and self disclosure is an open license of the fundamentals and principles of a certain type of the donation-based Crowdfunding model.

Crowdfunding demonstrated an amazing milestone of influence in early 2013. Since its cancellation a decade ago, fans of the cult-classic TV series Veronica Mars have been clamoring for a movie to sum up the show's plot. The franchise raised over $5 million in just 48 hours! While critics say its likely a rarer case for crowdfunding platforms, the power of the masses cannot be denied when it comes to making a popular vision a funded reality.

Crowdfunding Today

In the past year the concept of crowdfunding has matured and is now becoming mainstream. Today's Crowdfunding represents its own unique category of fundraising, and is currently a hot topic for startups, thought leaders, non- profits and inventors.

According to the "Handbook of Entrepreneurial Finance" (Schwienbacher & Larralde), the authors define Crowdfunding as follows:

"In simple terms, Crowdfunding is the financing of a project or a venture by a group of individuals instead of professional parties (i.e., banks, angels or venture capitalists). Crowdfunding occurs when entrepreneurs "tap the crowd" by raising money directly from individuals. The typical mode of communication is through an Internet Platform."

Essentially, Crowdfunding is the effort of a large group of people making small contributions to collectively fund a startup company - or any other worthwhile fundraising initiative.

Crowdfunding projects can range greatly in both objective and size, from artistic and humanitarian efforts to cultural and social projects - to for-profit entrepreneurs seeking hundreds of thousands of dollars in seed capital as an alternative to traditional venture capital investment. According to Massolutions, a research, advisory and implementation firm that specializes in crowdsourcing solutions for private, public and social enterprises, donation, reward and lending typically raise $5K or less, whereas equity campaigns boast at or over $190K.

Most entrepreneurs begin their voyage by tapping their family, friends and coworkers for the initial funds. Historically, this approach has, at best, produced marginal success. Furthermore, bank loans, institutional investors, private equity, angel and institutional equity funding are typically not available for startups. Another obstacle for startups (founders) is determining a way to get together with funders. Without some kind of exchange, only tech-savvy companies that have a Web-based business could raise money that way.

Since Crowdfunding is becoming commonplace, and the Internet has made international investing quick, easy and possible, let's next look at the global marketplace.

Global Overview

The world is continuing to adopt crowdfunding across many categories. As a result, it is providing access to a new source of capital for entrepreneurs in many countries. Additionally, crowdfunding is providing the opportunity to revitalize those in need. This said, North American and European platforms are still overwhelmingly dominant, raising significantly more capital than platforms in all other regions combined.

According to Massolution, North American platforms raised in excess of $1.6bn in 2012, which is a 105% increase compared to 2011. In 2011, the North

American crowdfunding market grew at the lesser rate of 86%. European platforms raised close to $945m in 2012, which is a 65% increase compared to 2011. Of the 536 platforms worldwide, these regions still account for more than 95% of the total market.

Clearly the trend of Crowdfunding is most popular in North America and Europe where many early adaptors and regulatory agencies have given the trend a clear approval. But other countries and regions are quickly catching up.

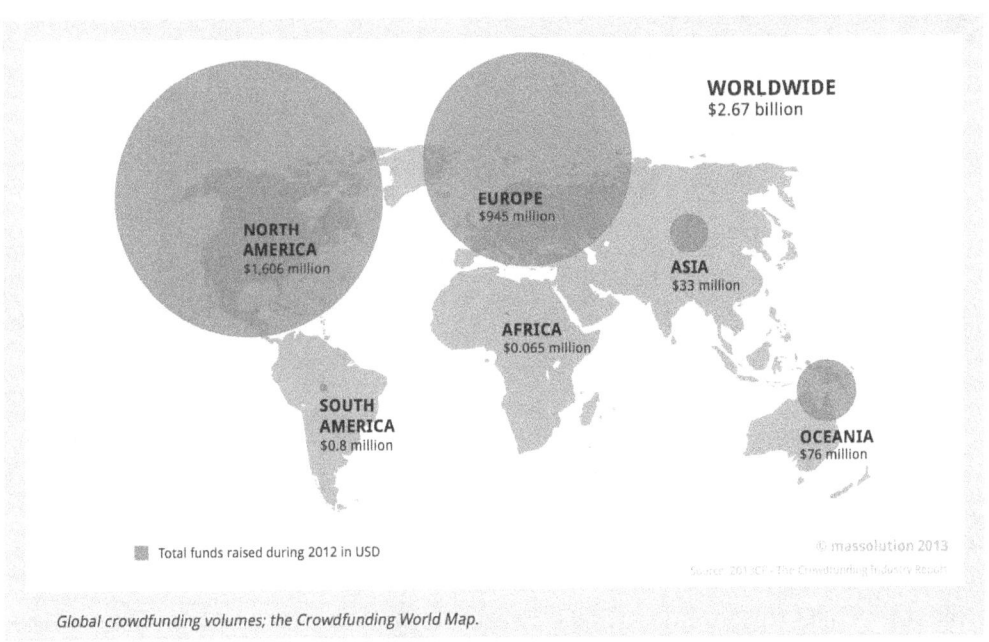

Global crowdfunding volumes; the Crowdfunding World Map.

Crowdfunding in Asia and Oceania is accelerating. Aggregate 2012 funding volumes are below $50m and $100m, respectively. South American and African crowdfunding portals, or CFPs, are also emerging and funding volumes are accelerating from a zero base at a much higher rate than other regions, where crowdfunding is more established. Moreover, the growth rate for South America and African CFPs increased from 2011-2012.

So while slow to get into the Crowdfunding game, these countries are embracing the Crowdfunding model faster than previously well established regions, such as North American and Europe. It is interesting to note that the different Crowdfunding models are well represented in the make up of this growth.

Of the amount raised, donation and reward based crowdfunding grew 85% to $1.4bn. These two categories are obviously the largest (and the easiest to get buy-in for). Kickstarter, Indiegogo and Crowdrise all follow this model. Lending- based crowdfunding grew 111% to $1.2bn. While "lending" is technically microfinance, this medium is increasing popularity across the board. Finally, Equity-based crowdfunding grew 30% to $116m. While this is practiced in many European countries, the SEC is still writing the rulebook for the United States. It is expected that this area of crowdfunding will skyrocket once it becomes legal.

Crowdfunding was first popular as a vehicle for funding creative and social

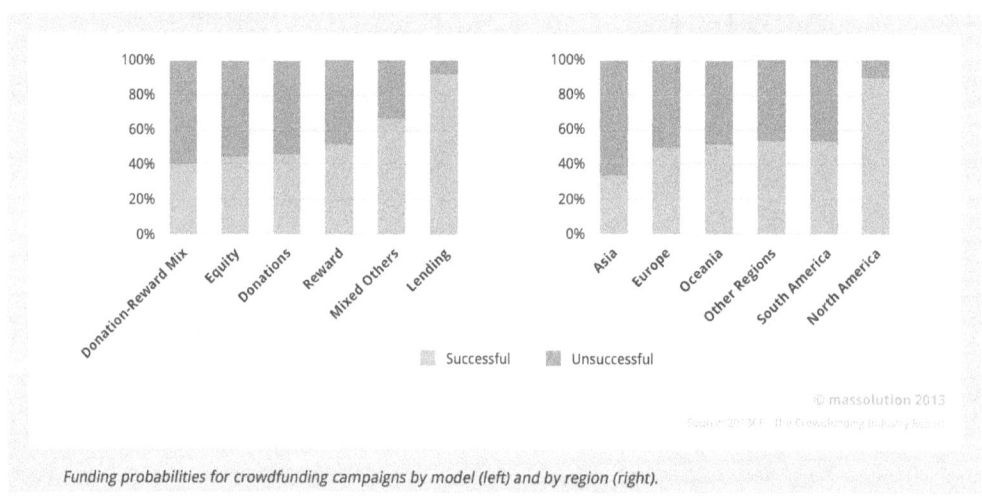

Funding probabilities for crowdfunding campaigns by model (left) and by region (right).

projects. While this is still true, entrepreneurial ventures have also gained traction in the industry. The categories have grown to include Fashion, Music and Recording Arts, Film and Performing Arts, Business and Entrepreneurship, Energy and Environment, Information and Communication Technology, Journalism, Books, Photo, and Publishing, and Science and Technology. Using models that generate financial return, the 'Business and Entrepreneurship' and 'Energy and Environment' categories are the next highest performing categories.

Social Causes are most active, driving close to 30% of all crowdfunding activity. This is not surprising given the prevalence of charity and donation-based crowdfunding. Business and Entrepreneurship (16.9%), and the two major Art Categories follow: Films and Performing Arts (11.9%) and Music and Recording Arts (7.5%). Finally, Energy and Environment (5.9%) is the emerging category among the five most active.

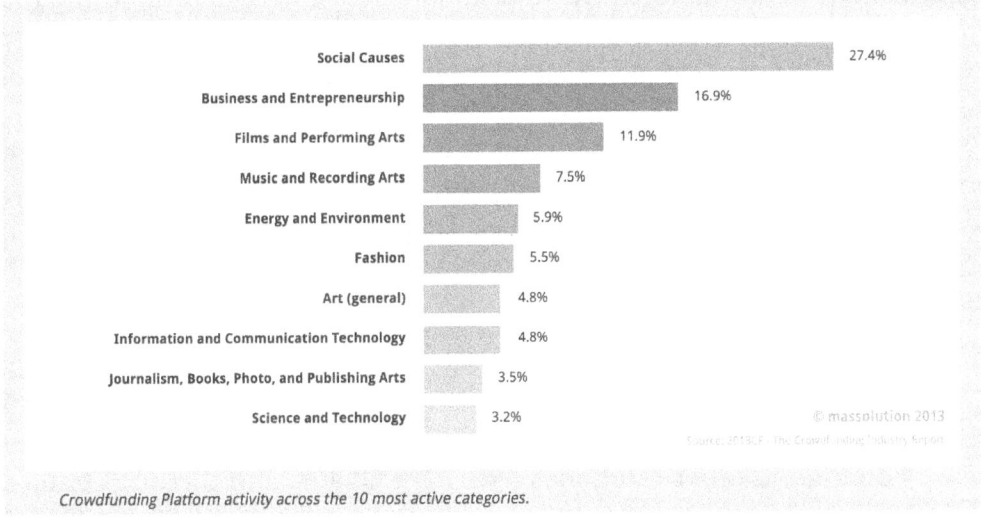

Crowdfunding Platform activity across the 10 most active categories.

Seeing that mainstream industries are working with the crowdfunding model, may offer validation to hesitant investors and encourage additional projects in other fields.

"Obtaining reliable and analyzable data on all aspects regarding new constituents- and market-related activity will be critical to the creation of the new crowdfunding industry... This includes more research on funding platforms, deals, investors, amounts being raised, actually raised, industries, and geographies. For the last several years, Massolution has committed itself to developing these necessary capabilities, relationships and infrastructure to be the best positioned and most reliable market leader for this purpose."

Douglas Ellenoff
Managing Partner, EGS

Ellenoff brings up a valid point. While all of these statistics are helpful, there is precious little data on the industry as a whole. These points give the business person an idea of where things are headed globally, but the direction of this industry as a whole has yet to be determined.

Back Home: JOBS ACT

America may be the leader in crowdfunding, but it cannot do everything that Europe can, due to the current status of the JOBS Act, the law that allows expansion of this new industry. Our associate at Massolution puts it best:

"While lending-, donation-, and reward-based crowdfunding have thus far been leading this global financial revolution, equity-based crowdfunding is about to take center stage in the U.S.... The JOBS Act, which will allow non-accredited investors to make investments in exchange for equity, is expected to go into effect by the end of 2014."

Carl Esposti, CEO, Massolution

"Crowdfunding" is the trendy new term in the high-tech arena, though it is well recognized in other categories. President Obama and the U.S. Congress capitalized on this trend to spur the economy by passing the JOBS Act. This act essentially requires the Securities and Exchange Commission (SEC) to adopt new regulations to Rule 506 of Regulation D mandated by the Jumpstart Our Business Startups (JOBS) Act of 2012. Section 201(a) of the Act requires the SEC to adopt new regulations that eliminate the prohibition against general solicitation and general advertising of private securities offerings conducted. This piece happened recently in early fall 2013.

The purpose of this provision is to facilitate capital formation for small business. Although the legislation required an implementation date, which has already passed. The SEC has proposed Rule for Title III that focuses on Crowdfunding, but they but have not gone into effect yet.

"Americans who want to start new businesses currently face many discouraging obstacles that have dampened the entrepreneurial spirit of this country and damaged a critical source of job creation. Since 2007, we've seen a 23 % drop in new business creation, according to the Bureau of Labor Statistics, and October's annual World Bank's Doing Business report found that the United States fell to No. 13 for ease of starting a business, down from No. 3 in 2007," Missouri Representative Sam Graves said in a statement.

Startup Act 2.0

Together with Startup Act 2.0 the climate and opportunities for entrepreneurship is becoming abundant as it relates to funding. The latter legislation, introduced shortly after the JOBS Act was signed into law, makes it easier for foreigners who obtain advanced degrees to stay in the United States after their visas expire. The concept is to make it easier for these individuals to stay after finishing their studies and start businesses in the U.S., rather than joining the exodus of foreign graduates (including American-born children of immigrants) with skills in science, technology, engineering and mathematics (the so-called STEM field) who return to their native countries, such as India and China, to jobs in their burgeoning tech sectors.

We are now witnessing what will likely become a new paradigm of investment opportunities for launchers of crowdfunding platforms designed for start-up funding for entrepreneurs, socially responsible projects and personal milestones.

> *"The JOBS Act will help address our recently declining entrepreneurial track record by providing opportunities, increasing capital formation and paving the way for more small-scale businesses to go public and create more jobs."*
>
> **Rep. Sam Graves (R-MO)**
> *Chairman of the House Small Business Committee*

The act has passed. On September 23, 2013, the first part of the JOBS Act went into effect and enterprises were allowed to solicit funds from Accredited Investors only. The second part of the JOBS Act allows the 'Average Joe" to become a venture capitalist for the first time in America's history. When the rules were finalized by the SEC the number of shareholders that a company can have increased tenfold.

Investors also found themselves in a unique "cusp" position. They can fund one or several companies as long as they remain within 5% or 10% of their annual earnings ($100,000). They must be registered as accredited. An accredited investor has an income of $200,000 and/or $1 million in assets. Moreover, an investor must wait 12 months before selling their securities unless the sale is to a family member, the issuing company, or an accredited investor.

As of today, recent changes in laws and legislation have only loosened the guidelines for how money can be raised. For instance, a company can crowdfund up to $1 million over a 12 month period ($2M with audited financials). So every year, a company can raise another sum of money for their organization. This same company can still use other funding sources. Lucky for them, companies crowdfunding are exempt from the 500 shareholder cap. In return, these companies must provide a description of their ownership and capital structure.

Beyond the Sea

While crowdfunding is still gaining momentum in the United States, we have seen this financial model experience significant success in other parts of the globe including Europe and Australia. In many ways they are ahead of the US.

In the United Kingdom, the platform Abundance Generation was the first regulated by the Financial Services Authority. It was approved in July 2011 and launched into the public scene in 2012. This platform provides debt finance to UK-based renewable energy development. Seedrs Limited launched among the first equity crowdfunding platforms to have received regulatory approval anywhere in the world. It was given the green light July 2012. This platform is pioneering for equity crowdfunding. It allows users to fund as little as £10 (and companies to gather up to £150,000 total) in exchange for equity. As a result of its success, the entrepreneur philanthropist Richard Branson announced his support of crowdfunding, and endorsed several platforms. Today, Seedrs Ltd. is one of the most popular platforms in the UK.

Sweden and Norway have also gotten a decent start on crowdfunding. FundedbyMe launched in 2012, featuring both donation and reward based crowdfunding. In early 2013, Invesdor came on board as an equity platform.

As you can see, equity crowdfunding has already been legalized in these countries, and has achieved wonderful success. China launched a large equity platform called SeedAsia to promote upstart business in the greater Asia area, and has now expanded to include the globe.

While it has existed for over a century, the last three years has seen a boon in Crowdfunding. Never before has this type of funding been possible with the magnification by Social Media. The industry is changing and evolving daily at the state level with regulations. There is constant opportunity to provide services in the industry and for ideas and businesses to grow and prosper.

INDUSTRY

CHAPTER
TWO

Overview

Crowdfunding describes the collective cooperation, attention and trust by people who network and pool their money and other resources together, usually via the internet, to support efforts initiated by other people or organizations.

According to Crowdsourcing, LLC, the total number of worldwide Crowdfunding Platforms (CFPs), as of April 2012 (when the JOBS Act was signed into law), was 452. It is estimated that the number increased to 536 CFPs after December 2012.

As we discussed in the previous chapter, North American crowdfunding volumes grew 105% to $1.6 billion in 2012. Globally, the 2012 worldwide crowdfunding volume reached $2.7 billion raised from over 1.1 million campaigns. Worldwide crowdfunding volumes grew 81% in 2012, which is acceleration from the 64% growth in 2011. Lots of people love to give: Donations- and Reward-based crowdfunding grew 85% to $1.4 billion in 2012. $5.1 was raised in 2012 in total for all categories. In short, this industry is here to stay, and is only getting bigger.

Myths Debunked

As with anything new, there will always be people who doubt the viability of a project. However, the proof is in the statistics - there is a long history of fundraising the United States and globally. Additionally, as with many industries, the Internet has been the catalyst for change. When we look at the video industry and how we went from retailers like Blockbuster to mailed DVDs like Netflix, to streaming video; we know that websites like Hulu, and YouTube helped get us there. The music industry is a classic example; Napster changed the way that we consume music, and then iTunes completely changed the game with its electronic devices and online store.

If history repeats itself, we will be seeing an influx of the crowdsourcing model in professional services, which includes the financing of ideas, projects and businesses through crowdfunding. Looking at the industry, which is still in its infancy, you will see there are already many stereotypes, myths and misconceptions as to what the industry actually is, and how it works.

"Crowdfunding (CF) is for starving artists, crazies, and misfit entrepreneurs"

This was perhaps accurate at some point, however, now it's actually a very lucrative model, and has been demonstrated as such. The average amount earned in a campaign for donation and reward based lending is about $5K, which speaks to the potential of money that can be moved in a campaign!

CASE STUDY:
LET'S TAKE TWO COMPLETELY DIFFERENT CAMPAIGNS, ONE IN MUSIC/ART, AND ONE IN HYDROPONICS

A music case study is "Emily the Strange" a Kickstarter campaign about a comic book character named Emily who was starting a band. The creator Robert Reger had a comic series going for years, but he decided to create a campaign that would help animate Emily's first "single." The campaign raised just under $65K in one month, with 710 backers. Reger had created a following, and used his fandom to make the single possible.

http://www.kickstarter.com/projects/1847107349/first-ever-emily-the-strange-animated-rock-n-roll

Changing gears, another project literally blossomed in the environmental area. Modern Sprout was started by a Chicago couple named Nick Behr and Sarah Burrows. Out of interest and necessity, they created one of the first (and most stylish) hydroponic planters for people's homes. This means a sleek planter that only needs water to grow some amazing plants. This team had a very strong video and were able to articulate what they were doing and why. It appealed to those interested in cooking, decoration, and of course, sustainability. The campaign raised $77K with 678 backers in just over a month. This team had a plan, and spent a lot of time preparing before launching their campaign.

It doesn't matter the "subject" or "category" of your product or service. If marketed well, any campaign has the chance to be funded well beyond its goals.

"CF is a fad"

Crowdfunding is only getting bigger and more disruptive. Once equity crowdfunding passes, it will skyrocket as the new paradigm of business. If you go back to our history and overview section, you'll see that this industry is only getting bigger, better and more value with a lot of potential for the entrepreneurs of America.

"CF does not work"

Quite the contrary, in 2012 there was $5.1 billion raised for projects. There are countless projects that have raised money that met their goal; started by people like you. This book will help you learn the keys to a successful campaign.

"CF is fun, but not lucrative in the long term."

Neither was using Facebook or Twitter to market a business. Now, it is a primary tactic for online marketing and digital growth.

One of our favorite examples of changing an industry's landscape for the long term is Uber. In 2010, Uber raised $1.25 million from various "super angels"(this is still a close cousin of crowdfunding). It is a ride sharing app that allows the user to text a car to arrive for transportation at a certain location. It is said to take on "taxiing woes." Founded by Garrett Camp and Travis Kalanis, the San Francisco launch was just the beginning. They've expanded over the past few years, and most recently secured $360 million in their latest round of funding. The crowd made this project possible and continues to drive its success today.

"CF is a scam"

Fraud is a serious issue present in all businesses, especially the upstart world. However, in many ways the transparent, public nature of CF actually   mitigates against fraud more than traditional venture capital.

Also note that crowdfunding fraud isn't even the biggest type. When it comes to credit cards, or "merchant retail services," there is greater worry. These figures are bigger than the current crowdfunding industry. In the Merchant Services Industry, they are processing trillions of dollars monthly, and there is only $8 billion in fraud. This represents hundredths of a percent.

Crowdfunding is likely to go even less than this theoretical percentage. Crowdfunding happens largely on Social Media. On these platforms, actions are so transparent as everyone is held accountable by reviews, comments and rating systems. On Social Media more than anywhere else, the truth comes out, and fast.

"CF is for young people/Millennials/etc."
CF is a tool available for anyone with an idea, or money to support one. But here's a little more information on the average statistics. In mid-2012, the American Dream Composite Index surveyed a sample of the U.S. population to establish demographics for general crowdfunding participants. Age-wise, individuals ages 24-35 were found to be much more likely to participate in crowdfunding campaigns; those over 45 are significantly less likely to back campaigns. When it comes to gender, men are much more likely to take a risk on an unknown startup. Finally, those earning over $100,000 per year are the most likely to invest in startups through crowdfunding. Keep these in mind when tailoring your message to your audience.

"I've thought about learning social media and CF, but it's going to take too much time."
It's easy to learn, and fun! This book will give you the tools. There are also portals out there like Funderbuilt™ that help bring the tools to the project, making it easy. These include messaging, publishing schedules, email management tools and Social Media publishing software. While fundraising does require time and sometimes money, the return is well worth the effort.

"Someone will steal my idea"
This is possible; however, with the right legal protection, you can protect your ideas and businesses. A service like Traklight (http://www.traklight.com/) can help protect and track intellectual property for an individual as well as a business. It is important to note that it takes more than just having an idea to generate value. Actually executing on the idea, and building demand for the

product or service it represents is the actual valuable. Additionally, it is healthy to have a little competition.

"Social media is undignified for my kind of project."

While crowdfunding can fund anything, it may not be for everyone. Crowdfunding requires authentic and trusted communication with a community and some projects cannot do that. Crowdfunding is a great solution to the need for money for ideas, projects, and companies, and provides a turnkey solution for raising funds in an efficient and effective manner.

"My project will just get lost in the noise."

Creating the proper brand and messaging will set the project apart. Additionally, with the right use of Social Media and Public Relations you can create awareness. The messaging, video and style with which you execute will help your project rise above the noise.

"People like to vote for winning things," agree Ariel Hyatt, an American music publicist, author, and Social Media strategist and Jonathan Ostro. "In your campaign, you don't want to come out of the gate weak." This means that to rise above the noise, your project, brand, and messaging all need to be very strong and clear before you launch. This is what "springboards" your project to attention and success.

"Social Media is a waste of time."

Put this book down right now, and pick up our other book, "The Simple Secrets of Social Media."

In all seriousness, Social Media is changing the way we do business. For the first time, marketing is a two-way, push-and-pull communication between audience and consumer. This presents an opportunity for businesses to get the best possible information in a very transparent, authentic and honest way.

We hope we've debunked the myths surrounding Crowdfunding for you. As you can see, anyone can raise funds by using Crowdfunding, but it's important to note it is not right for everyone or every project, and success depends on your willingness to do the work necessary prior to launching your campaign, no matter what type of Crowdfunding campaign you choose. Before we get to the steps you'll need to take, let's take a look at the different types of Crowdfunding campaigns.

Types of Crowdfunding

There are multiple types of Crowdfunding available depending on the type of project and the way the individual wants to contribute their money. To help illustrate this, let's consider a business example most of our readers have experienced: a lemonade stand. Meet Johnny, who is 9, and lives in your neighborhood. Using Johnny's Lemonade Stand, we will go through the list of the different types of Crowdfunding.

Donation Crowdfunding

Donation Crowdfunding is where a crowd of people (friends, family members, supporters, strangers, etc.) donate funds to a cause, idea or project. These small amounts from a crowd of people add up to something significant. A variety of donation crowdfunding platforms have emerged to allow ordinary web users to support specific projects without the need for large amounts of money.

In Johnny's case, you may pass by him in the neighborhood, and while you aren't thirsty, you'd like to support him, and hand him a few dollars. You have just made a donation to the lemonade stand, and Johnny can run his stand. You probably gave him the donation because you like him, his family, keeping kids off the street or just have a soft spot in your heart for young entrepreneurs.

CASE STUDY:
CROWDRISE ON WHY DONATION CROWDFUNDING WORKS

If you don't give back no one will like you

Crowdrise is a donation based crowdfunding platform started by actor and activist Edward Norton, producer and activist Shauna Robertson, and Internet entrepreneurs Robert and Jeffrey Wolfe. Crowdrise was named a "Top 25 Global Philanthropist" by Barron's and a "Top Fundraising Website" by Mashable. Crowdrise will not say how much it has raised total, but the pages on the site suggest the number to be at least several million.* They combine a well-designed site powered off the principle "if you don't give back, no one will like you."

*http://adage.com/article/digital/read-crowdwise-story-ll/232662/

When it comes to making crowdfunding actually work, Robert Wolfe claims a specifically dedicated email is the best approach.

"People rely so much on Twitter and Facebook to get the message out, but it doesn't convert well to actual donations being given. In this case, email is king." He goes on to describe emails as creating less noise and to have a much greater instance of a clickthrough rate.

Robert and his team have always been about making giving back fun. If people like doing it, they will do a better job. If it's fun, people will do it again. Crowdrise is designed to be viral and social, with a series of ranking, badges and points available to win and display on your profile based on the amounts of money you raise. Since about 78% of people make purchasing decisions based on peer recommendation, crowdfunding is all about peers giving to peers.

Ultimately, he believes crowdfunding is the way of the future because it involves customers driving the decision making. "When customers drive the decision making, they are more engaged, and better decisions get made."

Giving back has been one way to get the crowd passionate and engaged. We only see the influence of Crowdrise and other companies like it getting bigger.

Microlending (or Microcredit) as Crowdfunding
Microlending is the extension of very small loans (micro loans) to borrowers who typically lack collateral, and a verifiable credit history. It is designed not only to support entrepreneurship, but also in many cases to empower individuals and uplift entire communities by extension.

Let's say Johnny's parents give him just enough money to buy lemons, sugar, water and ingredients for any baked goods he might feature at the stand. At the end of the day, Johnny's parents might take back the $20 he made, plus a couple extra dollars as interest. While this is not ideal (or likely) for Johnny specifically, it can help many businesses get started. And he learned the value of OPM (Other People's Money).

Reward Crowdfunding

With Reward Crowdfunding, Investors get the satisfaction of helping an idea, startup or business through a financial contribution. In return, they get a pre-determined reward or perk of value, or other recognition, but no equity or finished product.

This is where Johnny's Lemonade Stand appears in classic form. You pass by it while walking in your neighborhood, buy a glass of lemonade or a pitcher from Johnny, and give him money in exchange. This is reward crowdfunding; your reward is lemonade for your contribution. If you had given more, your reward might have also included a cookie. Johnny's reward tiers were advertised on a chalkboard.

CASE STUDY:
GROOVEBOX STUDIOS AND THE WRECKING CREW FILM

The four partners at Groovebox Studios (GBS), Shawn Neal, Jeff Wenzel, Elise McCoy and Kevin Tuczek have assisted more than 100 artists to get funding through Crowdfunding for live sessions recorded in their Detroit studio. When documentary film director Denny Tedesco needed help raising funds for his film The Wrecking Crew, he turned to GBS and their expertise. As consultants on the project, the GBS partners built and managed the campaign; same as any campaign for any artist before, but this time they were leading a larger team and not going solo.

NOTABLE RECORDINGS

"Good Vibrations"

"California Girls"

"These Boots Were Made For Walking"

"Mr. Tambourine Man"

"River Deep - Mountain High"

"Windy"

"California Dreaming"

"Monday, Monday"

"Danke Schoen"

"Mrs. Robinson"

"The Beat Goes On"

The film focuses on the studio musicians working on almost all of the top hits coming out of LA from well-known artists, including The Beach Boys, The Carpenters, Simon and Garfunkel and were the key component's of Phil Spector's famous "Wall of Sound" in the 1960's and 1970's, with Tedesco's father, Tommy, being one of the key musicians. Other artists include Nancy Sinatra, Wayne Newton, Sonny and Cher, Brian Wilson, The Mamas and Papas, John Denver, The Byrds and The Monkees.

This group of musicians became known as The Wrecking Crew. Tedesco was able to get a special licensing for the songs used in the film with the caveat that he had to pay all the union fees, which amounted to a quarter of a million dollars. The GBS crowdfunding campaign was specifically to handle that last chunk, paying off the performance royalties to the musician's union, so the money actually went to the subjects in the movie, the musicians that played.

The GBS team managed the process and developed the strategy nine months before they launched the campaign.
The Wrecking Crew film is aimed at baby boomers and at the time, baby boomers were just discovering Social Media, so they could not rely on Social Media alone to drive the campaign. Instead, GBS had Tedesco do a screening tour to hit all the hubs and markets of support, and rallied his closest fans. He did a number of film screenings in that 9-month period, screening the actual film since it was completed.

While Tedesco did screenings of the film, the team spent the time lining up committals for celebrity tweets, from comedians, and LA stars and musicians. Neal's team generated a 'tweet package' for the celebrities; they had to use a specific link and specific five words, the rest they could fill on their own. Some posts generated $10K within an hour after tweeting.

"While we were certainly driving the boat, I think it's important to note that Denny had assembled a killer team of individuals to execute this plan. The quality of this team was instrumental to its success, especially when it came to rallying the support of celebrities and people from the music industry. One individual in particular, Greg McViegh of Guesthouse Projects carried much of that burden and hit home run after home run. Much of our advice and guidance in the nine months leading up to launch was focused on encouraging Denny to be patient and wait until he had his team in place. Once the team was assembled it was all about execution. Our advice alone would not have funded this campaign. The efforts of the full team Denny assembled and their commitment to following the plan is what made this project successful," said Neal.

The campaign ran for 60 days and in the first ten days got to about $50,000. "They thought it was over, and I was cheering and I was like 'perfect' it was exactly what we needed to do," said Neal. "We amassed 20% through email links; 80% were coming from his hard core most fervent supporters. After that support came from the celebrity layer. It was an LA movie that celebrates the industry in LA," said Neal.

"So it's really about these stages, about knowing who your best performers would be and what platform to use, and that in the middle other than leave it to die, we had to hit little fires that would spark amongst communities, that's where we back ended with all those celebrity tweets in the middle 40 days, and in the very end it was the momentum when the national articles started hitting, the Radio blitzes and we tied it up for the ramp up to N.A.M.M (the National Association of Music Merchants Show is the world's largest trade-only event for the music products industry). In the last days we raise about $90K that put us over the edge, it came down right to the wire," said Neal.

How did they do it? Neal says, "It was knowing the trends, spotting them before hand and having the strategy in place to know who we're trying to reach when we try to email, and the path these things take and having an answer for each condition you're going to be in." In the end, the target was $250,000; the goal was reached and exceeded with 4,245 backers; $313,157 in pledges and more that was given after the Kickstarter campaign ended.

CASE STUDY:
REWARD BASED CAMPAIGNS - GROOVEBOX STUDIOS & IAMDYNAMITE

There's something special happening in Detroit's Music Scene – Groovebox Studios (GBS). What make's GBS Detroit so special is not just that all of its music sessions are recorded LIVE in one room, by one band, in one take, they also help the bands fund the sessions through Crowdfunding.

Using the crowd the four partners, Shawn Neal, Jeff Wenzel, Elise McCoy and Kevin Tuczek have helped more than 100 artists fund their live sessions at the studio with an overall success rate above 90%. The projected budgets range from a few thousand dollars to hundreds of thousands of dollars. Groovebox's standard for running a successful funding campaign is fourteen days – a timeframe unheard of in the Crowdfunding Industry.

To put it into perspective, GBS' campaign development to in-studio session is usually 30-45 days. That means an artist contacts them, they run a campaign, get funding, and the resulting content is released in that short timeframe. Typically a GBS campaign is two weeks with approximately 45 backers; an average band raises $1800 – that is until IAMDYNAMITE blew the funding charts away.

The band's earlier attempt at funding through the crowd failed so the two members were hesitant to try again; they didn't want a black mark against them with their fan base. But Groovebox Studios had a plan – offer fans the ability to attend a live session as one of the rewards, and even offer a reward of house parties for larger donations. The fans of IAMDYNAMITE answered – they wanted to party with the band!
Instead of the standard fourteen days running a campaign, with IAMDYNAMITE, they

shut it off at day four and funding of $4,328. "We were at three thousand five hundred dollars in the first three hours!" said Neal. "They told us, 'oh my God it's doing too well, you have to slow it down!' so we basically zeroed out all the awards. "What peaked the interest of the crowd was the something only GBS brings to the crowdfunding arena – "unique access" to the band.

The unique access – allowing fans into the studio for the live recording party - and house concerts - generated more than immediate funds for the band, it generated deeper relationships. The house concerts were so memorable to the band they are still talking about it two years later. For one house party the band flew out to Tyler, Texas; the backer's teenage son was a fan of the band. When they set up to play there were only twelve people present and, as they were getting ready to play, the whole neighborhood showed up. Next thing they knew there were 120 people at this backyard pool party. "What went from being one teenager being their fan, an entire neighborhood became friends with IAMDYNAMITE. That neighborhood to this day talks about the day the rock band came down and broke the place," recalled Neal.

Recently a band member told the partners that two years later, a major label, after touring the world and global recognition, the band says GBS was one of the best experiences they ever had. Two years later they are still hearing from the fans, still hearing stories from the road, fans that came to the session are meeting up on the road and they have a more intimate connection. "What we did is we broke the wall for them, they now know it's okay to interact with a fan and know the value of that and have become completely different artists just from that little '$1200' campaign with us for a December 27 show in our studio," said Neal.

For more info on the campaign: *https://www.kickstarter.com/projects/gbsdetroit/gbs-detroit-presents-iamdynamite*

Equity Crowdfunding

This new model will allow large numbers of "regular" people to invest small amounts each online to fund early startups.   This is not a get-rich-quick vehicle for consumers. A small business can use this as a way to sell off a portion of their company in exchange for money.

Let's say a well-to-do neighbor sees Johnny's Lemonade Stand, and is impressed. So impressed, in fact, he sees Johnny opening multiple stands all over the neighborhood. In this case, he might front Johnny extra money to open the new stands, and recruit other kids to work, and the neighbor would then have a say on how these stands worked. He would also have his entitled share of the stands in dividends, of course.

Anyone wanting to do equity crowdfunding should first seek professional advice as it relates to selling equities and structure deals. Because legislation is being written at this time, a professional lawyer will be able to tell you specific policies and procedures in the current grey area, and any rules and regulations that need to be followed in this area.

With this recent change to crowdfunding, it has become more relevant to equity investors. Crowdfunding portals' reasonable steps and self-accreditation is not enough. The SEC has not yet defined what is enough. Third party companies like crowdentials.com are popping up to fill this need.

CASE STUDY:
CIRCLEUP ON THE PRESENT AND FUTURE OF EQUITY CROWDFUNDING

CircleUp provides a venue for accredited Angel Investors to network and fund projects. This is the closest form of funding to equity crowdfunding to date. When talking about the impact of crowdfunding on the financial landscape, CEO Ryan Caldbeck describes crowdfunding as a movement that will affect small business only.

"Big companies, tech companies...they already have hundreds of angel groups and capital chasing them. The only companies of this size that might use crowdfunding are those who have already been passed over by other sources." Because of the billions of dollars Caldbeck describes in the investor capital world, it seems that crowdfunding does little to fill a void here.

For crowdfunding to really work, Caldbeck describes two things needing to happen. The first is that the company already needs to have some capital in their possession. This shows investors the clout that they have and are capable of. The second is that "crowd" really needs to be able to understand and analyze a business they would invest in. For example, a biotech business would not have great chances of working because most people, the investor crowd, wouldn't have the capacity to analyze all the details and modeling of the business.

Caldbeck came from the Private Equity world. His two funds were retail-focused private equity at TSG Consumer Partners and Encore Consumer Capital. His experience in private equity exposed him to many great consumer and retail businesses that were too small to obtain funding through the customary private equity channels. As a result, he decided to make funding available to these smaller and promising companies through CircleUp. "Smaller" companies wanting to work with this network are described as needed a half million in revenue before applying. What's more, the network only takes <2% of people who apply.

When speaking to the future of crowdfunding, and how it will impact the big players on the financial landscape, it's up for debate.

"Everyone is guessing wildly at what these rules will look like. Investors might take advantage of it, or they might not care at all," says Caldbeck. While he believes the general rule that the smaller the company the better fit for crowdfunding it will be, there's a certain limit.

Direct Crowdfunding

CASE STUDY:
"DIRECT CROWDFUNDING" WITH LOCKITRON

One Friday morning in late 2012, the creators of Lockitron, an innovative deadbolt system controlled by your smartphone, were rejected by a major reward-based CFP on the ground that it is a home improvement project. As graduates from Y Combinator's 2009 summer class, the founders formed a plan in the following week: they would launch Lockitron's fundraising campaign on their own website and try to bypass the usage of a CFP.

Lockitron offered a direct pre-order mechanism that was risk free - the customer pays ($149 instead of $199 later) only when the product will be ready for shipping. It was a big success. In 30 days, the founders received 14,704 pre-orders totaling $2,278,891— success that propelled the company into the ranks of the most successful crowdfunding campaigns.

While most of the successful crowdfunding campaigns are intermediated through CFPs, Lockitron made a breakthrough by being one of the first tremendously successful initiatives that utilized a direct reward-based mechanism. Is this success indicative of an evolution in the crowdfunding marketplace, or will the next revolution in crowdfunding take a form more akin to the open source phenomenon?

The founders of Lockitron certainly think so: the team launched Selfstarter.us, an open source crowdfunding site offering entrepreneurs a generic skeleton and use of Amazon Payments to get their campaigns off the ground.

Selfstarter.us is crowdfunding at its most basic level: it frees entrepreneurs from paying the commission required by most platforms, serves as a pre-ordering payment gateway, and collects multi-use tokens from customers.

Crowdfunding today is a wide open space for almost infinite creation. Whether it's a platform, or a gray area project, there is a place for it.

Crowdfunding Alternatives

Praenumeration, mini loans, and crowd-sourced donations are all notable precursors to crowdfunding. As seen in the historical example of Grameen Bank, even the smallest loans can make an enormous example. The same goes for illustrating the impact of crowdsourced loans in the Statue of Liberty story. The modern concept of crowdfunding began its current growth with micro lending, and evolved to the model we know today.

Microcredit is the extension of very small loans (micro loans) to borrowers who typically lack collateral, and a verifiable credit history. It is designed not only to support entrepreneurship, but also in many cases to empower individuals and uplift entire communities by extension.

As you may have guessed, there are some great websites out there that facilitate this process. Some of the top ones are Kiva.org, which allows an investor to make a loan as small as $25, Grameen-Info.org, the pioneering bank from the previous section that still thrives in this modern setting, and CGAP.org, which provides financial solutions to the poor.

On the whole, this model is very altruistic. Not only does it provide a poor person or an entrepreneur a chance to create a sustainable living, it also cultivates choice for many people – they are able to choose the type of work they want to do. This model is unfortunately not without its flaws. The biggest of these is exploitation, usually in the form of the lender becoming a "loan shark," charging the entrepreneur ridiculous interest rates on the start up cash given. Also, the scope is pretty narrow. This model is mainly employed by nonprofits to help the poor. Because of this scale, many businesses and their startup requirements may not be a fit for this model.

Incubators

Business incubators are programs designed to support the successful development of entrepreneurial companies. This is done through an array of business support resources and services, in hopes that these will support the developing businesses enough to be "born" and flourish once it graduates the program. Incubators usually have strong networks and funding sources allowing them to support these companies. The way they deliver their services also varies, as do their clients/companies served. Typical support services include everything from marketing and presentation assistance to obtaining small loans or providing a workspace for the company. The average company spends about 33 months in a program. After graduation, a business is twice as likely to succeed.

There are a few drawbacks. First, they narrow the collective wisdom of the crowd. In other words, there are fewer opinions that matter focused on your project, and the feedback you get may not represent the market as a whole. For example, you might pitch an idea to all 800 of your Facebook friends. Instead of hearing from all of them, using an incubator would be like paying only 50 of them to answer, rather than casting a wide net and allowing natural selection to occur.

Incubators don't account or allow for scalability. When you enter an incubation program, it assumes a certain size to your business, and how much you'll be able to "supply" to the "demand" of the market. They will help the company build its machine. However, let's say you're ridiculously successful upon graduation, then you will need more machines, with an incubator environment, this is not what they are contracted to help you with, so the model is flawed in this scenario. Conversely, if you were to overestimate the market demand, an incubator may not be able to help you downsize.

Finally, incubators only focus on the seed-funding stage. Once a company has its upstart money, it's usually set free. While this may appear to be an advantage, if the market has "spoken" (i.e. doesn't pick up) the little guy can get hung out to dry. It also doesn't guarantee future funding for company expansion or growth. This issue can usually be out-leveraged by other forms of funding in the future.

See our Business & Investment Appendix for a list of the top incubators in the US.

Private Angel Investors

Private Angel Investors are affluent individuals who provide seed money for businesses in exchange for convertible debt or ownership equity. The capital they provide can be a one-time injection of seed money or ongoing support to carry the company through difficult times. Angel investors give more favorable terms than other lenders, as their motivations frequently go beyond money (more industrial, or seeing a specific dream come alive). They are usually focused on helping the business succeed, rather than reaping a huge profit from their investment. Angel investors also form into groups, pooling their resources and sharing their portfolio.

The term "angel" originally comes from Broadway, where it was used to describe wealthy individuals who provided money for theatrical productions. Being the "sponsor" of a show carried prestige and potentially big returns that could be reinvested if the show was successful. This practice has evolved to one where the very successful strive to continue their successful track record by offering expertise, experience and contacts, in addition to money, to help companies they relate to, succeed and grow. In 1978, William Wetzel, then a professor at the University of New Hampshire and founder of its Center for Venture Research, completed a pioneering study on how entrepreneurs raised seed capital in the USA, and he began using the term "angel" to describe the investors that supported them. This is what coined the name in the professional world.

http://www.unh.edu/news/docs/2007AngelMarketAnalysis.pdf

Not all Angel Investors are created equal. Some are very particular and want to be hands-on, others fly by the seat of their pants, investing in whatever seems interesting or inspiring to them. Most Angel Investors are accredited investors, which means that they have an income of $200,000 and/or have $1 million in assets.

Private Angel Investors aren't always a "go-to," however. Many times, they want more equity than the business is willing to surrender. Along the same lines, they also want to become decision makers, or amass some other power and influence. These are key issues that deter many businesses from seeking angel investors.

It should also be noted that Angel Investors do not usually provide for long term funding. Family and friends aside, most AVC (Angel Venture Capital) groups participate for one round of funding. Finally, there's a cap on the amount of funding an Angel provides, the range usually falling between $10K - $500K*. According to the Angel Capital Association, there are over 330 groups in the United States and Canada that are active within the startup community. Look at our Business & Investment Appendix for the top Angel Investment groups in the USA.

*http://www.angelinvesting101.com/Lesson%201.htm

"From where I sat as chief of the SEC's Office of Market Intelligence, I saw all kinds of microfinance fraud. My one key piece of advice to anyone seeking to finance a venture is to be careful to avoid those unscrupulous promoters, brokers and lawyers who are more interested in making a quick buck

than seeing your venture succeed."

Thomas A. Sporkin
BuckleySandler LLP

***

Family and Friends

Family and Friends are another classic source of funding. Perhaps it's your Great blue-blooded Aunt Bertha, or maybe that business school chum who has made it big. These people are mostly on your side, and have invested in you, the person as much if not more than the business. Family and friends can be helpful in getting preliminary buy-in for a business. If anyone is going to say yes, it is this group. Before you go out to the public, you need the support of your inner circle, your first degree. Even if you wanted to secure big investors for a project, it is likely that you'd need seed money, which would come from your family and friends.

Regulation D

You may have heard of people raising money for a project or a person investing in a startup company. This is traditionally done under exemptions to the registration provisions of the Securities Act of 1933. Private placements (or non-public offerings) are a sale of securities by the company directly to a limited number of investors, usually a bank, insurance company, some other large institution or high net worth individuals. These investors need to be cleared, but not registered with the SEC. Recent changes to SEC "Regulation D" have increased the number of investors a company can solicit and sell securities to without undergoing the costly registration process. But to take advantage of these exemptions, issuers must follow certain rules and be careful of who they are soliciting and who they are ultimately selling securities to (as previously discussed).

There are many advantages to using private placements to fund an enterprise. First, few prior assets or credit references are needed making the chance to get started quite feasible. Second, no SEC filing is required for the actual entrepreneurs. Finally, with proper professional guidance the process can be relatively easy. Typically an attorney can draw up the papers, and assist in the transaction including executing the documents. This is one of the cleaner/more realistic ways to get a business funded and is also the closest to crowdfunding to date.

Capital raised through Regulation D offerings continues to be large – $863 billion reported in 2011 and $903 billion in 2012. Only 13% of Regulation D offerings since 2009 report using a financial intermediary (broker, dealer or finder). The real estate issuers (REITs) use intermediaries the most (27% of offerings), while hedge funds use them the least (6% of offerings). This means that the market is indeed growing, and changing in a way that favors Crowdfunding.*

http://www.sec.gov/divisions/riskfin/whitepapers/dera-unregistered-offerings-reg-d.pdf

Regulation D establishes three exemptions from Securities Act registration. Each of these rules is very important when it comes to understanding (and using the "safe harbor" of Regulation D.

Rule 504

Rule 504 provides an exemption for the offer and sale of up to $1,000,000 of securities in a 12-month period so long as the securities are sold in a manner consistent with state law. General offering and solicitations are permitted under Rule 504 as long as sales are restricted to accredited investors only. This is more or less in congruence with what was stated above.

Rule 505

Rule 505 provides an exemption for offers and sales of securities totaling up to $5 million in any 12-month period. Under this exemption, securities may be sold to an unlimited number of accredited investors and up to 35 non-accredited investors. These other purchasers do not need to be completely versed in business or at a certain level of wealth. Purchasers must buy for investment only, rather than resale. The issued securities are restricted, in that the investors may not sell for at least two years without registering the transaction.

There are some requirements that come along with this exemption. First, financial statements need to be certified by an independent public accountant. If a company other than a limited partnership cannot obtain audited financial statements without unreasonable effort or expense, only the company's balance sheet, to be dated within 120 days of the start of the offering, must be audited. If the limited partnership is unable to obtain required financial statements without unreasonable effort or expense may furnish audited financial statements prepared under the federal income tax laws.

Rule 506

Under the 506 Exemption, a company can raise an unlimited amount of funding from an unlimited number of accredited investors and up to 35 sophisticated non-accredited investors (meaning individuals who have sufficient knowledge and experience in financial and business matters to make them capable of evaluating the merits and risks of the investment). The 506 requirements include: being able to raise an unlimited amount of capital (this is a benefit, not a requirement), being available to answer questions by prospective purchasers and meeting the same financial statement requirements as for Rule 505. The rule is split into two options based on whether the issuer will engage in a general solicitation of investors, or simply advertising to market the securities. If the issuer does not choose to generally solicit or broadly advertise the offering to entice funders, then the securities can be issued under Rule 506(b) to an unlimited number of accredited investors and 35 sophisticated non-accredited investors. However, if the issuer wants to use the new general solicitation and

---

Here are the 5 things entrepreneurs should consider when pursuing a Reg D or crowdfunded offering:

1) Consider using a legal team that has a strong background in traditional capital raising and private placements as well as one that is well-versed in crowdfunding. If you do, you will be confident at the end of the process that you've chosen the optimal form of financing for your enterprise, and you will be able to rest easy that all applicable legal provisions have been followed.

2) Think about the number of investors you want. Whether you manage a lot of investors at low price points, or a few investors at a higher price point, each model has its own particular advantages and challenges.

3) Think about the future state of your ideal capital structure. The manner in which you pursue your first round of financing

may impact future options.

4) Due diligence is crucial. Vetting third parties to whom your venture will be reliant, vetting potential investors, and comprehensively vetting your business concept are critical to minimizing potential misunderstandings and distractions as you get your venture established.

5) Make sure the disclosure documents accurately describe the venture for which the financing is being sought and make sure you are comfortable being bound by the words in those documents before you accept your first dollar of funding.

Thomas A. Sporkin
BuckleySandler LLP

advertising provision, then all purchasers must be accredited investors.

Accredited Investor Exemption

Section 4(a)(5) of the 1933 Act exempts registration of offerings and sales of securities to accredited investors when the total offering price is less than $5 million. To use this section, one is required not to publicly solicit or advertise the offering.

Strategic Alliances

Strategic alliances happen when companies create formal or informal partnerships between their businesses. A formal partnership may be a sponsorship for another company's event, or partial ownership of that other company. An informal partnership may simply be one company advocating for another online. These help generate goodwill, and credibility, all which help support a company getting more funding.

How does it relate to crowdfunding? It all comes down to the principle of strategic relationships between entities whether crowdsourcing or funding, key relationships need to be chosen and properly nurtured. The key with crowdfunding is that, sometimes, this principle applies to several more relationships to individuals, rather than organizations.

SBIC

Congress created the Small Business Investment Company (SBIC) in 1958. It was designed to facilitate the flow of long-term capital to America's small businesses. While the program does not provide capital directly to businesses, it instead partners with private investors to capitalize professionally managed investment funds (known as "SBICs") that finance small businesses. No tax dollars are used, but these private investment funds have the clout of the government.

The tough part is the application process to qualify for the program, but similar to grants (below) and small loans, can be very helpful for people who have few other options.

This said, it is a really difficult way to raise money, and is usually not for a start up. Businesses that are already established should consider this as a last resort.

Grants

Grants are a non-repayable sum of money issued from one party (usually an institution, corporation, or government) to another. The recipient is given the money after they apply for the grant, through Grant Writing.

Most grants are project-specific, and usually go towards a campaign, cause or the start of a new business. As with SBIC, the people receiving the money need to be sure that their vision is in staunch alignment with the goals and objectives of the grant issuer.

While free money is great, you have to work for it. The process is long and arduous, and there is only one round of funding. Grants are also typically given to some kind of social or charitable cause, but not always. This process has the potential to be a compliment to crowdfunding, but if you are a business, we

SOME OF THE SECRET SAUCE

CHAPTER
THREE

Successful Crowdfunding is made up of four key components. These are organizational and operational structures: legal, finance, branding & messaging and digital Public Relations & Marketing. We want to touch on each component (the first two are largely taken care of by the portal), and describe their importance for your project.

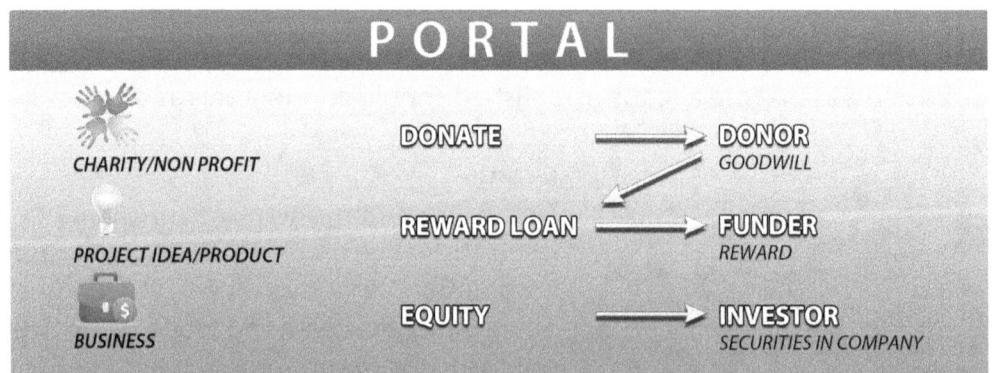

Legal

You can't sell what you don't own. Any asset (physical, intellectual or otherwise) has little value unless it is actually yours. This is one reason we have lawyers, to protect our Intellectual Property and creative assets. You can't rig the game. If you aren't sure how to protect or identify your intellectual property, firms like Traklight (http://www.traklight.com/) are good resources to use. The company's software will help identify intellectual assets, protect them and track them, making the process relatively painless. To rewrite the laws of business, you must first play by and master the current ones, then become the legislation you want to see. This can be tricky, and is another reason we have lawyers. Website and free legal documents do not constitute legal advice or replace the benefits of a licensed professional attorney, nor does it free you from your responsibilities to conduct your own due diligence.

Luckily, most of this is handled by whatever portal you choose to employ. They know what is legal, and what isn't, and will keep up on any necessary business standards on your project. For rewards and equity, think about your name and image; these are some basic creative assets. Do you want these to be protected? What about your Intellectual Property?

As we mentioned before, Regulation D is a huge part of the legality of crowdfunding today. And thanks to the JOBS Act, this is even more of a possibility.

Finance

We cannot stress enough how important it is for an idea, project or business to have funding. 90% of businesses fail in the first two years, with the most common reason cited as lack of funding. However, a crowdfunding campaign can help with this issue.

Every decision an organization makes has financial implications. The decisions you make to create the crowdfunding campaign display your capabilities in this area. We recommend that you start by listing out everything that you need to make your product or service work. Then, determine the "costs" of obtaining each item. Included in the cost should be money, number of people and time. The key decision that needs to be made is the amount of funding you need to raise. Price out expenses for your campaign, and how much reward fulfillment will cost. See our Financial Worksheet in the Appendix. Every dollar counts.

Managerial goals may be different than shareholder goals. Herein lies the value of equity Crowdfunding...there are way more shareholders than managers! This means that it will be important (essential) to listen to your funders. Be sure to let them know where the funds are going with a Sources & Usage Statement, and perhaps projections. This will add transparency, and as a result, credibility.

Branding & Awareness

Many classic marketing concepts apply very effectively to this innovative edge of business:

"Branding" was a huge 90's phenomenon. Everything was about making the business have a look and feel that is unique and recognizable. This would help businesses stand up above the noise. From this idea also came a way of commodifying the relationship of customers. Brand equity (how much clout a brand has over others selling a relatively similar product), and brand loyalty (customers consciously choosing one brand over the other, despite relatively similar substitutes) became a huge focus for business competitors.

On the whole, the best brands achieve these goals by delivering a positive experience to their audience. People can relate to a cause or need, sense the motivation behind the company, and feel moved or think on any messaging that they receive. When this is done well, action is taken. It is important to have a brand, either your product, services or you have to be the brand.

The first and most obvious is publishing. Whether its an advertisement, Public

Relations, or simply well executed market research, understanding your market and getting a clear concise message to a target group of people is key. Delivering the message happens through publishing. It's all about the content, how it's produced and distributed. For crowdfunding, this will mostly happen through Social Media or email (to be discussed in a bit). However, the content you create (project creative, pictures you post, your logo, etc.) should definitely be well thought out with a creative pizzaz.

The entertainment factor is also crucial in all of your marketing materials. Whether they are pictures or video blogs, it is important to both entertain and educate your audience. This is what creates engagement. The entertainment factor is how you can reach an "average" Internet user and reaching them will allow for sharing.

Marketing

We define marketing as a clear and concise message delivered to a targeted group of people. For the purposes of crowdfunding, this is best achieved by using Social Media.

Social media is a primary marketing and messaging tool. In this part of the equation, it can be used to stay connected with **frequent users** (people who regularly utilize your products/services), **funders** (people who fund your company), and **fans** (people who have/are/will advocate for your project, cause and/or business). It will be valuable to your project to acquire more of all three types.

The days of "push media" are gone - no longer can you provide one-way messaging to an audience. Today's media requires two-way communication which involves listening and speaking coupled with experiential marketing. Modern Social media platforms can provide all this functionality and much more. According to a recent Razorfish Consumer Experience Report, 49% of web users have made a purchase based on a recent recommendation they received through a Social Media platform. This is the executor of your crowdfunding campaign.

Using Social Media

There is a basic assumption that every business needs to make - marketing will create sales and therefore more marketing will create more sales. If one does not believe this as a foundation for a discussion on Social Media, there is no discussion. Assuming you understand the importance of marketing in your business, and therefore your Crowdfunding campaign, then you will understand the role Social Media plays in the process.

Social Media (a blog, Facebook, Twitter, Google+, Pinterest and Instagram) are all channels for producing content for your target audience to consume and engage with your campaign. These targets typically connect with you through Social Media in one of two ways: either they are on Social Media and begin consuming your content or they were introduced to your campaign in some other traditional capacity and transitioned into Social Media.

Once they are in Social Media, a campaign manager can use their channels to create trusted and authentic content that a community member will grow to know, like and trust with the end result being a consumer (and target for your campaign) that is loyal and more likely to take action the next time there is a donating or investing decision that involves your product, your charity, or your business.

When working in Social Media, we recommend using our framework outlined in "The Simple Secrets of Social Media," but in case you don't have the time to read it, here are a few of the key components...

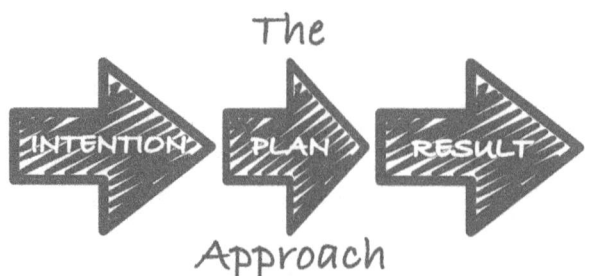

Intention: Why are you Engaging?

Why are you on Social Media? What is the purpose of your campaign? What is your intention for being here? More importantly, why should the audience be interested in what you're saying and take action because of it?

For many projects and companies, this can be scary and frustrating...what if we have this great idea for a product or a cause, and someone doesn't like us, or see value? What if we promise funders something and we are held accountable? What if you pitch the project to your audience, and it does not go over well? Some would say these are bad things, but great business people know the opposite to be true; these couldn't be more helpful. These "setbacks" will assist you in stripping away anything that is unessential to your vision and business. They also make for great practice and communications skill building.

Plan: Are you Creating Connections and Building a Viral Message?

The project needs to have a purpose, it needs to have a compelling message that people would know, like, and trust. This message should focus on the goals of the project and evoke action because the community believes in the message based on knowing, liking and trusting the campaign.

Creating a Digital Solution includes Social Media Optimization (SMO). Within each of these areas are sub categories in which we execute initiatives. For instance, in SMO, there is the use of Facebook, Twitter, Wordpress Blogs, YouTube and other Social Media bookmarking sites. Your efforts in SMO will improve the relevancy of your campaign.

By creating a strategy that is effective and efficient, you will achieve the results you desire. With a specific strategy in place, you and your team can execute and produce results. On a daily, weekly and monthly basis, these results can be measured against benchmarks and metrics that are set out as part of the strategy. Utilizing the latest in Social Media technology, you can manage your Social Media strategy ensuring its effectiveness.

Once you have connected with these people you will create trusted and authentic communication through gathering valuable, relatable and educational content that inspires people to get excited about your campaign, and fund it to fruition.

But content isn't enough, you must respond, and quickly to the questions, concerns and requests of your constituents. Remember, Social Media is just that, social; it is a conversation in cyberspace with your target audience. It must be two-way and as immediate as possible, or your supporter will seek out another campaign that is more responsive.

Result: What is the Goal for the Strategy

You measure what you want to affect - do you care about the amount of money, number of donors, average amount of donations, viral reach of the campaign? Give your campaign a target, a purpose and driving factor behind the effort. Through use of Social Media and the various platforms you seek to convey the message that will inspire individuals to become a part of the brand or cause you're representing. The efforts to create this message include interacting with target audiences, industry influencers and their families and friends.

At the end of the day, it is easy to write an article or make a post or even snap a picture, but without these key components, social media might end up just being what you had for lunch as opposed to producing supporters for your campaign.

CASE STUDY:
ECO EXAMPLE PROJECT

For example, let's take two women, Liz and Ashley Greene, who are wanting to build a community eco-home. Each has their own passion for the environment, has heard of and seen some really cool homes built to various effects. This home will be used by the local community as a learning and sustainability center, complete with classes, a community garden, and a volunteer network to "green" the community. But first, the building has to be built!

When they conduct their social media campaign, they listen to their community. What are people most caring about? What are the latest trends? As they listen, they begin to give great quotes and articles. This increases their followers and establishes them as an authority in the greening/eco area. They might also connect with people who have built, or are interested in becoming involved with the building of an eco home. The **INTENTION** is to be a part of the greening, eco-home movement, and also provide an outlet for community improvement. This has appeal at a national level, but also especially on the local level. The **PLAN** is to take 90 days; share designs, recruit different talented people to help with various aspects. Liz and Ashley also might create bi-monthly video blogs or updates as they begin pre-building the project. On these video blogs, they might interview different designers and architects, or even environmental scientists on what it takes to create a sustainable community. These pieces should generate interest, credibility, fandom and most of all, funds. Finally, when measuring **RESULTS**, they might both look at not only funds raised, but also audience engagement, video blog viewers, and feedback on their project and posts.

No matter your project, the Social Media process will position you more thoughtfully in the digital scene. This will assist you and your team in garnering more monies for your project.

CASE STUDY:
ARIEL HYATT AND CYBER PR

Ariel Hyatt started her voyage into crowdfunding when she published her first book, "Cyber PR for Musicians." With great success to this title, she has gone on to publish two more books, continuously building her expertise in the area of digital branding, social media and cyber PR.

When it comes to a crowdfunding campaign, Ariel states that people need to know that it's not to be taken lightly. It becomes a full time job. The ideal clients she works with are those that are willing to do the work along side her team, to see the project to success.

At first glance, it might be easy to think that PR and crowdfunding go together easily, but Ariel has a different take. "PR only merges with crowdfunding if the person involved is 'PR or press-worthy...most of the time, the traditional PR about a campaign happens after the fact, and usually only if the campaign has been successful.'" "PR-worthy" people are described as nationally known leaders or celebrities. Amanda Palmer is often cited as a leader crowdfunder, but Ariel brings up the point of her being an outlier "in the best possible way." Amanda has spent a decade building an intense, close relationship with her fanbase. Not even all musicians can brag about this quality with their own fans.

For the average person, the best and still very effective way to start is recruiting from their own "tribe." With the right niche networking, a person can start connecting with other similar tribes. "There are plenty of statistics that state that most funds raised for anything come from family and friends. The same can be said about crowdfunding." With this idea in mind, email is the best place to start, even phone calls. While social media is good for sharing updates and information, it isn't really a place where people get out their credit cards. Pre-plan tremendously. Ariel states that people like to vote for "winning" things, so having raised a lot before you start crowdfunding will help support this.

Finally, Ariel acknowledges a new type of risk associated (subconsciously or not) with crowdfunding: the emotional. Crowdfunding demands complete vulnerability to be successful. Any fear of rejection, acceptance, or not being "worthy" happens for people. "It's an emotional rollercoaster."

Pre-planning, and starting with family and friends will go a long way to helping people be successful in crowdfunding. Stick with your "tribe" and go from there.

GETTING STARTED:
Business Plan

CHAPTER

FOUR

For any project, even a successful charity event, one of the keys to success is to have a plan. It may be a one page document, but have a plan. When you know where you are going, it is easier to tell others (anyone who is going to donate or fund a project, wants to support a cause, a movement, a product) the purpose with a plan.

We keep talking about plans because they're so important. If you are doing an equity- or reward-based campaign, you should have a business plan already in the works. Outline your goals, objective and ideal timeline. Where do you want to be as you launch the campaign? Post campaign? A year from now? It is important to get clear and focused on your trajectory.

Typically, a business plan also includes a company mission statement, history of your group, and some well-thought-out finances. We stress this particularly for reward or equity campaigns because crowdfunding is first and foremost a business. People may want to give big, and a business plan will ensure them that you have thought about each part of your organization.

Preparing a crowdfunding campaign is a pretty substantial time commitment. While it is very easy once launched, it does require some planning and a lot of upfront work. As the old adage goes, anything worth having typically requires some work. Look at it this way, you are raising money to fund your next business, maybe your career or event a lifelong dream - so what are you willing to sacrifice to have this?

In the time leading up to the launching of your project, there are certain things you are going to want to do. We have outlined some of the bigger aspects of the planning that you should take into consideration.

Study other projects

There's no need to reinvent the wheel. Scan as many platforms as you can, look at profiles and watch promotional videos. Even if a campaign has nothing to do with yours, ask yourself: would I give money to this group? Why? The answers to these questions will help you get clear on how you want to present your own project to the world. Look at other projects! Get a sense for what has been done, what's been successful, and specific factors that brought that business success.

Prepare Assets in advance

We're talking as many as possible. This list should include your video, your business plan, and perhaps a sample/prototype if that's what you're selling. Additionally, you are going to want images for posting to Social Media, quotes, testimonials and maybe even some endorsements to use during the campaign to engage with your audience. Once the project gets started you need to be in execution mode and searching for these creative assets will be difficult. Crowdfunding is going to take a lot of your time and effort, so it's best to be prepared with these other time-consuming items, as quickly as possible.

Become "Pitch Perfect"

In 30 seconds or less, it is your job to be able to fully convey what you and your team are up to, and why people should help fund it. A pitch can be used for your video, it will guide some of your communications to prospective funders. In the business world this is known as an "elevator pitch." The key to getting this business pitch down perfectly? Practice. Practice using the bathroom mirror (seriously!) until it's second nature. Get some honest feedback from your family. Either way, this pitch needs to be crafted and ready.

To ensure your pitch is complete, make sure you've answered these key questions:

1. **What is your goal?**
2. **What do you do?**
3. **What is your unique selling point?**

These are all essential components of a pitch. Once these have been put together, all you need is practice.

Plan your rewards

If you are doing a rewards-based Crowdfunding campaign, know what you'll be giving to whom, and for how much. While the tiers may seem arbitrary, be sure you're planning out the costs of rewards with the amount of funds you receive in any given pledge. Each tier should correlate to the amount that you have been given. For example, let's say that you are a musician and are raising money for your next album. Your reward tiers may look something like this:

> **$5 Pledge - You're awesome, thank you for your pledge!**
> **$10 Pledge - Exclusive First Download of New Single**
> **$20 Pledge - First Download and Band T-Shirt**

While this is a pretty simple example, it is up to your team to decide how much you need, and what you feel you can really give to these backers for funding your campaign. Each tier should provide a motivation for the funding target, prompting them to want to give more, and more!

Project budgeting and completion

Be sure that you have enough seed money for the campaign, and ask enough to cover all possible costs. What is the cost to manufacture? What is the cost of using a portal? What is the cost of professional services, such as legal advice or an accountant? There are many services and items that go into securing and thriving on a great idea. These costs can pile up, so it is important to be clear on all essential items. Check out our Financial Worksheet in the Project Prep Appendix.

Funding Targets

Think about whom you'd like to get to hear your message. What do they want to hear? What do they value? Messaging to these people, specifically will help you secure a maximum amount of funding. I am sure that some of you out there are saying that you are not sure who you can ask, check out the list we've prepared below of potential funders.

List of Potential Funders

Here are various groups of people you might consider asking when creating your crowdfunding campaign. Notice the types of people here are pretty straightforward and are accessible once realized.

1. **Family Members**
2. **Friends**
3. **Friends of Friends**
4. **Community Members**
5. **Interest-Based Organizations/Groups**

Campaign duration

The average campaign duration is 91 days - 1 to launch, and 90 to strategically message and collect funds. We recommend that you create a campaign that is 31-91 days long. Any longer than that can make it difficult to achieve success for multiple reasons:

1. Most funding occurs in the first 7 days and last 7 days
2. It is more difficult to keep engaged with someone via social networking, emailing and texting for longer than 3 months and
3. When you have a well planned out campaign, you can make things happen rather quickly and things go viral without much effort.

Set Your Profile Up for Success

Now it's time to set up your actual profile on your crowdfunding portal. By now, you should have researched and chosen a portal that fits with your project's mission and goals. While most platforms officially fund "everything," notice which projects seem to be the most successful and on what portal. For example, Indiegogo features a lot of movies and performance artists. Kickstarter has much of the same, plus widgets, gadgets and consumer products. Fundperk has branded "swag" for any organization, and Crowdrise gives to charity only.

Choose wisely based on your project's needs.

Your CF campaign brand should match or correlate with your company's other Social Media pages. Take note of whether the registration is free or if you have to pay for the crowdfunding portal - is it worth it? When it comes to photos, include pictures of yourself and your team. These don't have to be professional, but should be well-lit, high-resolution, and nice looking. These will make you relatable to your funders.

Think of yourself as a creative agency with one big client: your campaign. For example, Moncur Associates is a small to midsize creative agency that specializes in high-end branding and messaging. One of their biggest services for clients is called "integrated online awareness." This involves both search engine optimization as well as an active Social Media presence. The key is to keep the content of their clients' sites as relevant as possible. This means telling a well-crafted story on an ongoing basis. On Twitter and Facebook feeds, they don't just publish to make noise. They engage their followers with exciting content that they may want to consume. Some content is planned (e.g. "30 days to go!") and some is spontaneous (e.g. "look at this crazy office happening!").

Running your campaign Social Media sites with an agency mindset, including both organizational and creative aspects, is another way to keep your project at the top of the rankings and top of mind.

RISKS & COMMON PITFALLS

CHAPTER

FIVE

"If you don't understand people, you don't understand business."

Simon Sinek

Avoid the Big Blunders

It's Not About YOU

When people start a business, they typically think they have this great idea, and are instantly off to market it to the masses. This approach typically fails because little research was done about what people really value. When it comes to crowdfunding, the same logic applies. Your success is based on the crowd and its wants, needs and desires. So, what do they value? What are their interests? Additionally, by listening to your crowd (audience), you can better understand them and ultimately engage them in the most effective way.

This Isn't Rocket Science

Your project, product or service may have a wide variety of technical components. Maybe the coding for software needs 3 types of developers on it (and hence funding to pay for these), or perhaps you need a particular type of camera for the type of film you're creating. The audience doesn't need to know every detail. Being too upfront with technicalities may be disengaging. Be thorough, but make your content digestible to all readers. If a potential really wants to know the exact process, they will ask. Be sure you have that answer ready too. People consume information when it is easy to digest - it is no wonder the USA Today is written at a Tenth Grade reading level*. This is not because most of its readers cannot understand more complex literature, but rather, it is meant to be easy to understand, a quick read and ultimately something that someone can relate to, remember and hopefully share with their network.

http://www.impact-information.com/impactinfo/newsletter/plwork15.htm

Audience Assumptions

There's a classic assumption in business that no longer applies, even remotely. It's called "build it and they will come." Stemming off of previous ideas, listening to your audience is going to be one of the biggest and best things you can do for your campaign. In a Forbes article, rock star Amanda Palmer stated that the 10 years of an authentic, honest relationship between herself and her fan body were what made her crowdfunding campaign so successful. In May 2013, she raised $1.2 million for her new album from over 25,000 fans. While not every artist or entrepreneur commands these numbers, it's about mobilizing the people who are "true" to your cause or project.

An audience is never a given; it is built. So if you are going to build anything, it would be an audience. What if you don't have an audience? Work with others who do...use PR and Marketing...take time to build one.

Who is in your audience?

There are many people that you can look to for resources during your project. Whether they provide time, money, assistance with marketing or even just your support, know who you are reaching out to.

FAMILY	FRIENDS	WORK	OTHER
Parents	Neighbors	Boss	Associations
Siblings	High School Classmates	Secretary	Clubs
Extended Family	College Acquaintences	Co-workers	Athletic Clubs
Children	Anyone you are connected with on social media	Vendors	Doctor
Church groups		Networking Organizations	Past investors/ funders
		Suppliers	Dentist
		Clients/Customers	Local government

Coming Up Short

It can be very typical for people to "perfectly" price out their widgets based on costs. But what if more than one version of the widget needs to be made? What about the shipping costs for reward fulfillment? All of these little details and scenarios can add up, and come back to bite you if not accounted for. Additionally, remember to subtract the processing fees of the crowdfunding platform and transaction system. Each usually take about 5% off of the funds that you receive at any given time.

Take a look at our worksheet in the Project Prep Appendix. Something similar to this will allow you to plot out, item-by-item, every single possible cost associated with creating your product, start to finish.

Risks

There are plenty of risks involved when doing a crowdfunding campaign. We have already mentioned the risks of reward fulfillment costs, and the large fees that a platform is able to charge. Along the same vein, you should be wary of reversed, failed or rejected pledges. There are many transactions that float in limbo, never touching a company's bank account. While this isn't necessarily the intention of funders, it does happen frequently enough, so even if you're close to being funded, don't stop until you're well over the top.

Other risks associated have to do with development. Some products will need testing, measuring and surveying. This not only costs money, but could also take a lot of time to get right. If your product or business has a lot of creative assets that need to be created, this can also be a necessary expense you may not have included in your budget. Whether it's composers or designers, the time and money investment for good creative is worth it, but needs to be included. The best option here is of course to get someone on your team with these skills, and who will put in a little "sweat equity."

Finally, operating costs such as overhead, office space and any salaries you might be paying in the future need to be considered. If you have to set up a corporation to have ideas and intellectual property that need to be protected, we recommend hiring a lawyer to cover some basic legal services.

It's better to set the bar higher and campaign even harder than to "hope" you get over funded, or the risk of getting underfunded. Nobody likes to dip into savings. Another risk is to deliver the wrong message to the audience. You need to speak to people who are open to listening to you and have an interest in your project.

On Failure

"Leadership is about moving from failure to failure without losing enthusiasm along the way."

Winston Churchill

We chose a quote on leadership because that's what doing a crowdfunding campaign is...pioneering into the unknown! Industry experts have called crowdfunding the "Wild West of business financing," so nobody has executed a perfect campaign. Rather it is an opportunity to lead a mini-movement, to create some organization amongst a vast network of people out in the crowd.

However, there are lots of insights from failed campaigns that you might use when creating yours, mitigating your own risk of failure. The first is a lack of a trusted brand, authenticity, well-known personality, and/or lack of a compelling vision. These are the essential drive behind a campaign. If you can't put your full "heart" into it, you really have no (actual) business doing it in the first place. The risk here is going through the motions towards a goal or brand that is not authentically yours, and wasting a lot of time, energy and resources in the process. This is a key insight from other failed campaigns.

Another set of failures comes from campaign owners not clearly explaining or illustrating a project's core value proposition or benefits. Your idea may be the best out there. But if it's not communicated clearly, explicitly or effectively, you may as well be silent. This is a basic that many projects do miss, confusing and disengaging potential funders.

CREATING YOUR MESSAGING

CHAPTER

SIX

While you may have the best idea, project or company, and perhaps it includes a great product or service attached with amazing creative assets for your branding and messaging, if you are speaking to the wrong audience, you are missing your target.

Sure you will get some money from your family and friends. However, to fund serious dollars, you will need to have a process for communicating with a larger audience and in order to get the action you want, you will need to get "in their head" to understand the energies that motivate their action.

In a framework created by a team at Harvard Business School, the Jobs To Be Done idea postulates that in every business interaction or purchasing decision, we "hire" and "fire" products everyday. And behind these purchasing decisions are various types of energy that move someone to make a decision. The ability to play to these will allow you to have more success with your funding. Additionally, there are different types of crowdfunding opportunities that will come into play here as well.

Chris Spiek, co-founder of Rewired Group (www.rewired.com), a creator of the framework, describes this as going beyond common sense. The classic story starts with the question of: steak or pizza? You might say that you like both. Most people do. The last time you had a pizza, you were probably watching a movie with your family. However, if you were to replace that pizza with filet mignon, things wouldn't exactly match up. This isn't because the filet is "wrong," but the context of the family watching a movie is more conducive to eating pizza rather than steak. Understanding context is key. Being able to understand your audience and the context will allow you to be successful with your messaging and ultimately your campaign.

Another example of context are the Milky Way and a Snickers candy bars. At first glance, these seem like two synonymous candy bars. However, you might have noticed that they are marketed completely differently. When asking people what they might replace a Milky Way with, the answer might be ice cream, a cupcake or soda. In other words, a luxury sweet. For a Snickers, responses gathered looked a bit different. These were a sandwich, a power bar, or a protein shake. Snickers to consumers equates as a meal replacement. With this in mind, messaging for Milky Way may be about enjoying a moment of luxury with yourself. For Snickers, it'll be about satisfying hunger on the go. Both are similar, but given their contexts, the messaging is completely different.

In the case of a donation ask yourself, what made that person part with their money? Why did they choose a Charity A vs. Charity B? Well, if we understand the "jobs" that people want to fulfill through a donation, funding a project or investing in charities, we have taken a step towards understanding the motivations of a given funder. With this you create more effective messaging: "if you give to us, the outcome you desire will be fulfilled." To do this, we need to know where the energy driving these choices comes from.

Before you officially launch, be sure to reach out to your family and friends first. Like any other rally or party, people don't like being the first ones there. When you host a big event, you don't just post a Facebook status the day of the party. To make the evening a success, there is preparation, legwork, creative decisions, and a close network of guests who are already coming. Maybe 25 guests have already agreed to help out. They'll be committed. With this kind of preparation (and, of course, stellar execution), you can achieve a real "hit" that leaves people wanting more. This same type of readiness applies to a successful campaign launch. Your family and friends will definitely support you in getting early funding (and referrals lined up).

There are essentially four types of motivating energy that drive an Internet user towards funding. They are Emotional, Social, Obligatory and Aspirational. Emotional energy is driven by how a product (or what it represents) intrinsically moves somebody. This might look like somebody being moved to donate to disaster relief due to a personal connection. Social energy is extrinsically driven; we act based on how others are acting, will act, or how we perceive/ are perceived. For example, someone might get an iPhone just because all of their friends have one. Obligatory energy is an extrinsic drive that people act on because they feel like they have to. In this case, maybe you sign up for your child's bake sale at school because all parents are expected to, even if it's not something you particularly want to do. And finally Aspirational energy is intrinsically driven. It represents the vision of how somebody wants the world to be, or how they want to be in it. It's the drive that people use to make dreams come true.

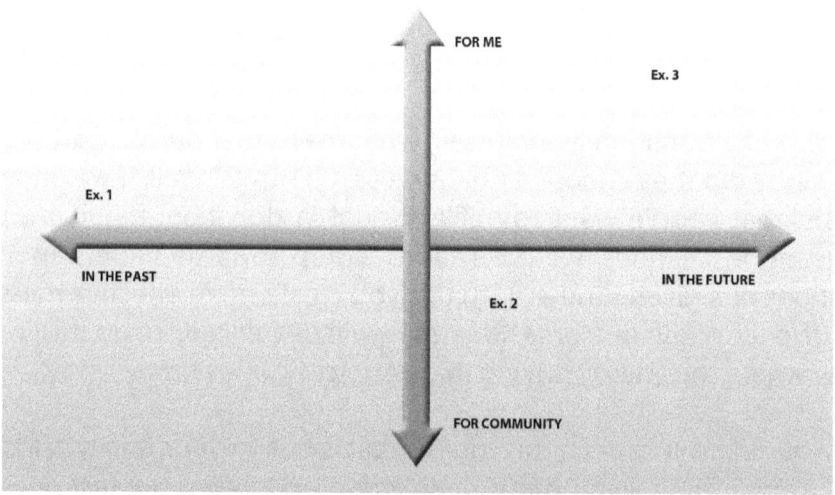

Now, let's take a few various decisions and put them on the diagram for your understanding.

1. Let's say one campaign is about cancer research. The team has beautifully executed their cause, and has run a great campaign. What makes them give?

In this case, it's something that is in the past and perhaps personal. Usually the funder may have survived cancer or had a family member who was affected. And it would also be positioned towards the community. The energy levels here are pretty transparent. It's the emotional ties to cancer that are the main driver to give. People also want to ensure others don't have to go through the same fate.

2. Perhaps another campaign is geared towards relief for an area that has been struck with a natural disaster.

This is more towards the center. It's happening now, and there seems to be a push and pull between how a funder is personally moved (karma, etc.), and how strongly most feel socially for the relief of immediate suffering for people. This ranks similarly for a situation like the Boston Bombing or Oklahoma Tornado disaster.

3. Let's say the producers of some epic canceled show decide to fund a sequel to round out the story.

It's both personal and in the future. While someone isn't necessarily moved by it at a deep level, it's really exciting, and quite aspirational to fund "the movie of the future." This is something their friends want to be part of and give to as well.

When thinking about your project, ask yourself which of these energies is more likely the driver behind giving. When collecting from your family and friends, ask them the thoughts they had behind clicking that button. With this information compiled, then you will be able to tailor your messaging to these various drives.

Once you have your messaging, test it with your family and friends. They can give you feedback and practice in your direct messaging and other communications about your project. Ask those closest to you - what makes them want to donate or fund? What got them excited? Answers to these will help you fine-tune your messaging.

Now apply this to your crowdfunding project. Even if your idea may have some viable substitutes there is a niche spin that you can capitalize on in your messaging. For example, if you have a gadget that allows you to easily find and track household items, you might try invoking an aspirational-type energy, with your basic message being "wouldn't it be great if you never lost your keys?" Never losing one's keys is something many might wish for. The essential concept here is to draw how the real value of your product or service, and design messaging that is compelling.

CREATE YOUR PROJECT

Answering these will unlock the potential in your project. While you won't be conveying them directly in your messaging materials, they serve as the building blocks for everything written and spoken during the campaign. We recommend you pick up a pen and paper, and jot down ideas that come to mind in this section.

Why should people give you money?

People work hard for their money and have many things to spend it on, so why should they consider you and your project worth letting go of those hard earned dollars? Ask yourself, what is the value in the cause? What is the motivation behind this entire campaign? What is your intention for changing the world? It is so important to answer well, because otherwise, the campaign has no backbone or foundation.

How are you helping people?

People want to feel like they're making a difference. Whether it's a donation to a really worthy cause, or a product/service that will include them in this feeling. Tell them how you are "living your dream" or your project is "making a difference."

What makes you different?

This is the real kicker - how are you rising above the noise? Your video should help be an outlet to illustrate this. Conduct your own SWAT analysis, show your project as a worthy cause, pull on the heartstrings of your target audience.

Do you have the skills?

Demonstrate that you know what you are doing, you know the market, the players, the potential of your project. Why should we believe you can do it? Give the potential funders a sense of your background, and make sure that your team's skill set covers all of what's needed to complete your project, and deliver to your funders.

How will you get paid?

Perhaps it's that feeling of doing "good," perhaps this new business is your livelihood. Really consider what you are investing in this project, and what you expect your returns to be.

Were you able to get clarity and capture all of your ideas?

The Basic Things

When beginning on your project platform of choice, it is important to have certain preliminary items known or handled. The list below should be part of the pre-launch phase of your project; use this list when uploading information for to your portal of choice. Use this step-

by-step guide to make sure your project is on its way to being ready. The Basics will depend on the type of project you do, but these should be enough to get you started.

- **Project Name** - Make it grabbing, memorable. This is likely to be the first thing they see.

- **Categories** - Choose only one category otherwise you may confuse the crowd. Those interested will find you and you won't dilute your message.

- **Name of Organization** - If your project is part of an established organization or corporation, you will be asked to specify not only the name, but the legal form of the organization (such as C-Corporation, Partnership, Charity, etc.) and if the organization has an Employer Identification Number (EIN) or not.

- **Project Ownership Information** - This to for the contact information of the person ultimately responsible for the project and the person the portal and the crowd will be in contact with directly.

- **Short Summary** - A short blurb about your project. This is going to be very similar to your elevator speech that you'll share in your video (below), but can be a little more wordy and formalized. Be able to give the basics of your project in 150 words or less!

- **Full Description** - People need to know exactly what you're up to. What is your story? Include your personal story (of you and your team members). Share with your viewers the events, drives and interests that got you to create this campaign. This should hopefully make viewers feel like they relate to you.

- **Financial Goal** - List the monetary goal of your campaign; how much money do you want to raise through the campaign. Be sure to work the budget and include all aspects, the costs of running the campaign on your chosen portal as well as securing and shipping any rewards.

- **Start and End Date** - Your portal will want to know when you want to start your campaign, and your supporters will want to know when the campaign ends. Do not begin your campaign until your plan is in place, your budget has been reviewed, your timeline is spot on – you won't want to be forced to stop the campaign because you weren't ready with any of these key components.

- **Business Plan** - A Business Plan will help your supporters and those wanting to invest in your project understand the direction you plan to take the product/company. Even if you do not have a full blown business plan, it is important to have the concepts and strategies articulated in a document to create a plan of action.

- **Financial Projections** - When you ask for trust and money, it is not totally unreasonable to be asked to show the projections for the product/company. If you state you will grow by 5% in a year, show how that relates in correlation to your business plan and what the projections are in revenues and expenses.

- **Pictures** - An image is worth a thousand words! Make your project personal, show your target audience who you are, who is in your team, where you work and live. Let them know you are credible and your ideas viable. Images of iterations of your product can be helpful to follow your vision of your product/service, etc.

- **Video** - Your video is critical and so important that we cover it in detail in our Video Appendix. The video may be your only opportunity to capture the interest of potential supporters, to educate them about your project, you and your team. Take special care when making your video.

- **Website** - Your website is another way to convey to your supporters and target audience that you are credible and real. Make sure your website is up to date and any details as they pertain to your project must be current and relevant.

- **Press Coverage** - If the press has written about you, your company, your leadership, products, services, processes, people you've helped, your story or project, be sure you have that information on your campaign portal to increase your credibility.

- **Project History** - If your project was created to complete something that was started prior to the current campaign, be sure you show the history of the project and how it got to where it is today. Include images, quotes, milestones and if you hit them earlier than projected.

- **Company History** - A simple history of your company will demonstrate many things including credibility, longevity, and financial stability. Be sure you highlight milestones of the company such as moving to a larger, new location, manufacturing additional products, strategic partnerships, key customer wins, key members joining your firm, patents, copyrights and Trademarks secured, etc.

- **Proven Track Record** - Running a company, being a successful entrepreneur gives you a personal history and track record of success. Were you a founder in a company that was later acquired? Can you show how your revenues grew and by what percent? Can you demonstrate quality leadership through employees who have been with you from the beginning? Have you successfully launched other projects? This is your opportunity to brag.

- **Management Bios** - Your chosen portal will have an area for you to upload the bios of your management team. Supporters will want to be sure your team has a history in the area of your project, education and practical experience that will benefit the project. If you have well known advisors involved, list them as well.

- **Logo** - Your logo will be key. This also needs to be grabbing, memorable, and reflect the story and pitch that you share with your audience. The best logos are very simple, clean and thoughtful.

- **Reaching Your Supporters** - The portal you choose will want to make sure you can reach your supporters and will most likely require you to list if you have an email list, including how large it may be, what your Social Media sites are and the reach of each as well as if you have a blog and press coverage.

- **Rewards** - Rewards are VERY important so place special attention to them; with the wrong rewards, no one will fund your project. Think about items that are valuable and that you cannot buy in retail commerce. Think about "packages" you can put together. Remember that people want value for their commitment to your project. Be sure to have your rewards thought out and at what dollar level of donation they apply to; are you limiting the quantity? Be sure to do the pre-work on your budget to know how many of the rewards you will need to reach your goal for each tier.

- **The Facts** - Finally, let them know the facts about your project. Include the dates that you are funding. Include your fundraising goal, and the suggested amounts for funding. With this should also come your reward tiers - what will people get in return for their contribution, if anything? State these very clearly, and be sure you can follow through with what you've promised.

- **Banking Information** - Where the funds are to be deposited. For Donation and Reward projects, there will be Merchant Services that handle the transactions.

There are many sites offering support for projects, in particular, we like sites that provide these tools for the user, such as Funderbuilt™. They help the project owner through all the steps necessary to create and manage a successful project. Their flexible funding model caters to the different types of projects (reward, donation, and equity-based) and the site offers a toolbox that includes the necessary guidance to using the tools. These tools include video creation outlines, ideas for spreading the word about the project, tools for tracking the progress as well as a simple vetting process.

Your Video

Your video presents an opportunity to grab your funder's attention: their first investment in you and your project. To start, we recommend that you examine at least 5-10 other video pitches, even if they are way out of your project's field. We have provided a list of questions to ask in learning from this process in the Video Appendix. Be sure to review them prior to completing your video.

When designing the video, we recommend that you keep it short, about 2 minutes or less. This parameter will help you get to the nugget, and viewers will appreciate it. Make it eye-catching. Be sure you have flattering lighting (want to appear "warm" to the camera), and are filming in a space that compliments your project and has the right "feel." For example, if you were creating a gadget, grandma's living room would not be the ideal space. A modern office, or even a science "lab" has the more correct feel.

When discussing your product/service/project, get to its value - what are its key selling points? This messaging should be clear, understandable and smooth. You want your talking to be authentic, rather than too polished or "professional." Make sure you tell your viewers why you're passionate about your project. This will give them reason to believe. Rehearse your pitch until it becomes second nature.

We also have a comprehensive list for how to craft your story. Remember, unlike other business pitches, this video could be viral in your investor community.

YOUR PROJECT LAUNCH

CHAPTER

EIGHT

Pre-Launch

The previous section's questions have helped you draw out your vision for this campaign. Then it walked through some basics of profile setup and video making. With these you're ready to go into the official pre-launch phase!

The Crowdrise website does a great job at making donations fun. As stated earlier, their saying is that "if you don't give back no one will like you." This fun, motivating approach is among the many things that has made this platform and its projects a success. Consider something similar when you craft your own messages.

This phase of the project is a critical phase. This is where you research and finalize your budget, your elevator pitch is ready, your video storyboards were drafted, your video produced, you've already gotten feedback from your family and friends, you've researched other projects to make sure your project resounds with your target audience. You've also enriched your Social Media reach, making sure you are reaching your target audience and your followers are primed to spread the work. You've taken quality images for your project portal and to include on your Social Media sites and you've updated your website and biography.

You've also planned out by the week, day and hour how you will keep your project top of mind with your followers, the media, and important people in your industry. Once your plan of action, and all your 'to do' items on your list are completed, then you are ready to launch. This process takes a lot of time to plan, but once you've built your own personal model, you can re-create it in future projects to come!

If you are not sure you are hitting everything you need to get done prior to your project campaign launch, check out our Task List in the Project Prep Appendix at the back of this book. We outline what needs to be done in a typical Crowdfunding campaign.

Launch

With a band of loyal fans, barkers (someone who promotes a project frequently across online venues) and funders, not to mention early seed money in the door and final campaign messaging tweaked, you are ready to launch. We suggest throwing a fabulous launch party.

This is the time to post on Social Media frequently - ask questions, let people know how excited you are, ask them to share your story too. Add updates and comments on the actual portal and encourage your supporters to add their comments too. Social Media is not just limited to Twitter, Facebook and LinkedIn. If you are making a gadget, get it on Pinterest. If there's a story attached to your product that lends itself well to a case study for an industry, submit it as a guest blog. The more online and mainstream exposure you can get, the better. Reach out to local radio and television with a press release and don't forget the newest press release is only 140 characters!

Remember, when you launch the timing is key. If you launch at eight o'clock in the morning on a Tuesday, you'll have the campaign ENDING at eight o'clock in the morning on a Tuesday. Make sure you give yourself time to get those last minute dollars in the door, so be tuned into the time and day of your launch and end of the campaign!

Keeping Top of Mind During the Slow Period

The beginning of every campaign has donations and investors, and then the campaign slows in the middle, and then picks up again at the end. That is the cycle of a Crowdfunding Campaign. Make use of the slow time by planning in advance communications to your supporters and non-supporters. Reach out to appropriate media, celebrities, industry groups, anyone you can think of that may be interested in your project! The worse that can happen is they don't participate in your campaign.

And during the course of the campaign, it will be important to follow up with various groups. These include the people who have already funded, those who are fans and are still interested, and maybe also people who haven't heard about your project yet. Each message should be tailored to that audience. For instance, you might give investors/funders the inside scoop of what's happening, and complete your message with picture updates, video blogs/podcasts, and other fun messages. These messages should be prepared well in advance (during the Pre-launch Phase) so you can simply send as you need them. You can also prepare special messages of thanks to your supporters as we've outlined in the Social Media Appendix.

On the other side, for fans or the general populace, you might share a surprising result ("Wow, our growth has doubled in the past week!"), or make customer reviews/feedback public. This should show them what they're missing. They will see that progress is being made and want to participate too! The goal is to share, and include selling points in your content (without being too pushy). When you get closer to the end of the campaign, remember to advertise that last final push!

After The Campaign Ends
No matter the results of your campaign, be sure to always follow up and thank your funders. These are the guys that helped you get to where you are. Depending on the rewards you used, now is the time to deliver. Ship or email out the goods, and be sure to ask the user for any feedback on the actual product or service. Thank them again in your rewards email.

When it comes to the actual money, it all depends on which portal you use. For Kickstarter, your project needs to have raised all of its goal money and more for you to get it. For Indiegogo, your project will receive any amount of funds you raise. Other portals are somewhere in between.

Be sure you communicate to your funders specifically where the money is going, and how it's being used. If you communicate well with these funders, and show you are putting the money toward the items you promised at the outset of your campaign, they will be more likely to fund future endeavors.

Beyond communicating, respond quickly to any inquiries from a funder about your project. Quick response will show them that you care about their point of view and by addressing their concerns you will demonstrate great customer service and promote good will.

Samples of Facebook and Twitter Posts are found in Appendix III. Use these as a starting place for your communications to your supporters and funders.

TIPS & TRICKS

CHAPTER

NINE

There are many details that go into making a campaign successful. Our experience has shown us time and again that there are things you can do to help ensure a successful campaign. We've listed what we think are the key tips and tricks for a successful campaign.

Keep Your Project Relevant

Do an Internet search for items in your industry, and see what lands in the top 10. These sites have the most relevant content out there. How can you adapt to your project? Is there a phrase or topic that you can speak to make your project more immediate and relevant to a viewer?

Fund to 40%, the Tipping Point of Success

Statistics have shown that projects that are funded to their 40% point are more than twice as likely to receive full funding. Do everything you can to get there, even if that means lining up family and friends as the first to fund your project.

Ask for Referrals & Recommendations

As you create messaging for your campaign, always ask for referrals and testimonials. Getting people excited enough to tell their friends will increase your exposure exponentially.

Don't Get Married

...To any one thing about your business. Usually the crowd will give you feedback; take time to listen. Whether it is the logo or various aspects of the service, accept that parts or your business are going to change, and that's ok.

Shipping and Reward Fulfillment - Outsource!

Shipping can be quite an undertaking. Outsource it.

Survey Your Supporters

Also, send a post-campaign survey to all backers (product preferences, etc. if reward), follow-up with all backers is key. Moreover, knowing their experience will allow you to improve upon your own process in the future.

Improve Your Chances of Funding: Creating the Basic Message

If there's anything you take away from here, do these things; first make a convincing case - cut to the chase, be persuasive, and clearly state why such a unique opportunity exists. Second, validate your approach: what makes it singular and successful? Also, what are your credentials?

Time is Running Out

Next, show funders that time is ticking. This should create urgency in their action. Finally, transcend the project. Or, link it to a larger picture, cause or movement.

On Launching

Be mindful of your days of the week, and when people are most likely going to be online. In Brian Fargo's case, 5am was not an optimal time for the audience his team was targeting.

"One big mistake we made was launching on a Tuesday at 5 am. When you launch determines when your project ends. Maybe it would have been better set at another day and time, like 5pm on a Friday. We could have had a great final day and a closing party. We could also have promoted that last opportunity to pledge...those final hours. But not on a Tuesday at 5 am."

Brian Fargo, Wasteland 2

Learning Curve

"If you don't fail at least 90% of the time, you're not aiming high enough." This

Alan Kay quote applies to crowdfunding, and how it should be approached. 46% of campaigns succeeded. Your first campaign should by no means be your last. Remember that this is a learning curve.

Start Today!

E Pluribus Unum, Gang Warily & Carpe Diem! These are all funny sayings on paper, but lend themselves as final pieces of advice for a great crowdfunding campaign.

First, it's not just about one company or person anymore. Right on our country's dollar bill is the phrase "E Pluribus Unum," translated as "out of one, many" OR "out of many, one." How does this apply to crowdfunding you ask? With this new medium, many people can fund one great company. One person can fund many companies. Moreover, these people and companies can collaborate as they wish, creating unprecedented synergy. When it comes to a campaign, continuous engagement is the key to success, you never know who could be your biggest supporter.

Channeling Braveheart with this Celtic phrase, "Gang Warily" reminds us to be mindful through the campaign. There will be ups and downs - these are natural, however, stay the course, remain focused. For example, most funding happens at the very beginning or the very end of a crowdfunding campaign. Remember as you go that the details need the most attention. People will notice. Always be sure what you're publishing has that personal, authentic touch, and that you've really thought about what you've sent out.

And finally, Carpe Diem, or "seize the day!" There is no better time to start your project than now. There is so much out there waiting to be invested, created, communicated and used. Crowdfunding can help facilitate this process, and is your carte blanche to personal and professional success!

INVESTING IN A CROWDFUNDING PROJECT

CHAPTER

TEN

We have covered crowdfunding from the point of view of a project manager, of the team launching the project. We have tried to clearly outline how to create a dynamic and compelling campaign, and honestly show the work involved before it launches, through the launch and after the campaign ends. Each step is involved has a direct impact on your bottom line, and if your investors will reinvest in your next campaign.

Now, lets take a moment to look at the other side of Crowdfunding, the investor side. If you plan on investing in a campaign, you need to know what the risks are and go into it with your eyes wide open.

What Should You Be Asking?

Backing a crowdfunded project can come with some risk particularly if the project is funded but fails to make good on its perks and promises. What should a backer know before investing in a crowdfunded project (including risks), and what financial questions should they be asking?

What is interesting about raising money in this day and age is that with the advent of Crowdfunding, there is a new funding source in town - the crowd. Family and friends and their family and friends can become your new investors and bankers. With this paradigm shift, some of the more traditional requirements have loosened, but some of the same risks still apply. There are a few key aspects to consider prior to backing any project.

Do I believe in the project?

Start by asking yourself why you are investing in the project. Seek to understand what about the project you like. What about the project attracts you - the cause, the product, the project owner some other reason?

A good test for this: would you share this project with family or friends via email or social media?

Do I believe in the project owner?

Every project has an owner - the person who took the time to birth the project and create the profile on the crowdfunding platform. Sometimes this is an individual, other times it is a small organization or community that believes in the cause or product or service that they are promoting.

This person usually tells the story about the project, they are also the person the money will go to at the end of the project to use the funds toward the intent of the project being promoted.

A good test for this: would you be proud to endorse this project so that others could support the efforts of the project owner?

Would I be OK if I never got any return on this project?

While most ideas (and projects) start out with the best intentions, Murphy's Law kicks in and there may be some reason why the original intention that one sets out for, changes or ends up being snaffled. Therefore, whether making a donation, contributing to a reward or investing in a company, you must always be prepared to receive no return.

A good test for this: are you were willing to take the money and give it away to a stranger with no expectation of them ever returning it?

Conducting Due Diligence

One of the first steps to lessen your risk is to always conduct the proper due diligence. Whether you are looking at a reward, donation or equity based project, there is a certain amount of due diligence you will want to conduct in order to ensure the deal is what it says it is.

For a donation-based project, you are going to want to ensure the cause is legitimate, which is as easy as a Google search. Additionally you will want to see if the project is in line with your personal values.

For a reward based project, even though you might like the project you are going to want to better understand the manufacturing of the product, as well as the history of the management team. This should be provided in the project profile or through a Google search. If you are averse to investing in any product that is not manufactured in the United States, then you are going to have to make sure this product is not manufactured in Asia, India, or South America.

As for equity based projects, traditional funding sources want to see that the business or idea will make a return on the money and the ability to scale the business, so these are usually a good place to start. Additionally, the management team is key to the execution of the plan, so it is important you feel comfortable with the people involved.

Gathering this information can be accomplished through the project profile or through a Google search. Check to see who is on their site as an advisor, how many employees they may have to show stability and growth.

Lastly, it is important that the project can demonstrate a detailed business strategy, and that there are growth opportunities or an exit strategy in the market, as well as a management team can be trusted to execute on the plan.

Vetting Through The Crowd
One of the main benefits of Crowdfunding is that the crowd works as an aggregate to vet the project and ultimately to be the peer recommendation or credibility to the outcome of the project.

It is important to see how others are interacting with the project - are they giving and if so how much? What types of rewards are they claiming? How many funders have taken action on the project?

In addition to others' interaction, it is important to determine where they are at in their project - Would you be an early funder to the project? If so you should have an intimate knowledge with the project owner or the cause, product or industry. Is the project almost over? If so, how are they doing towards their goal? How close are they to reaching their goal? Are they over their goal?

Lastly, it is necessary to watch the conversation around the project. Look at the Social Media channel for the project and see how the owner is interacting with the community. The Social Media sites for the project should be listed clearly on the portal. What about the comments on the project profile - are they positive or negative comments?

What Platform Are They Using?
When looking at projects it is important to look at the portal they are using - is it a reputable platform? Are there other projects on the site or is this the only project? Does the portal have the tools necessary to assist a funder in properly conducing due diligence on a project? What does the portal do in the case of a fraudulent project or scam? Does the portal address this in their FAQ?

It is important to make sure you understand the logistics of the funding transaction, as well as the security of the portal. A good test: look at factors like how many projects are on the site, how much money has the site raised, has the site received media coverage and if they have credentials such as an SSL certificate, BBB stamp of approval, and the type of funding processing they are using, such as PayPal.

Do I trust the place that introduced me to the project?
At the end of the day Crowdfunding is about the crowd and the viral nature of peer recommendation. As the message around the project is catapulted by the volume of the crowd more people will hear about it and ultimately the goal should be for more people to contribute to the funding. With that being said, it is important that you personally feel comfortable with how you heard about the project.

A good test is to ask the person who shared the project with you if they have funded the project. If you read about the project or saw an advertisement, do you trust the source that provided you the information?

What Does Your Gut, Infinite Wisdom Tell You?
You ask most people why they did something and they tell will you "it just feels right." Sometimes you just have to go with your gut and let that be what guides you in making a funding choice. Even after doing all the things mentioned above, sometimes you just have to go with what feels right to you. If it looks too good to be true, than you may want to walk away and if something is not

adding up or there is a red flag, then you need to listen to these feelings and hold off on the project.

As for investing in projects, know that for every great project you hear about an investor making, there was another 3-4 that did not work out. It is how investing works, no one talks about the ones that fail, they talk about successes. As with almost anything in life, if you are able to have a 30% success rate, you are doing something right most of the time!

NEXT STEPS

CHAPTER

ELEVEN

The next step in your journey is to check out our programs. We have many ways you can learn and tap into the entrepreneur knowledge base and eco-system.

THE TREP TALK BLOG

Entrepreneurs are the focus on The Trep Talk blog (*www.thetreptalk.com*). The site is a reservoir of relevant information that is useful and practical for entrepreneurs, with contributing writers from a variety of fields and experience. It also has all our upcoming live events including webinars, seminars, keynotes and MeetUps.

If you are interested in having Michael S. Melfi speak to your group, please contact *anne@melfiassociates.com*. If you'd like to be a contributing/guest writer, please let us know at *info@trepsnest.com*.

THE TREP TALK PODCAST

Learning from other, more seasoned entrepreneurs, is a great way to avoid the missteps that can come when you are just starting out or facing an obstacle you may not know how to overcome. The Trep Talk podcast on the Michigan Business Network (*www.michiganbusinessnetwork.com/blog/author/the-trep-talk*), hosted by Michael S. Melfi and Rod Hairston, showcases a different entrepreneur weekly. The questions are consistent, but the answers vary as much as the individuals and their businesses. Yet, they all faced challenges and obstacles as their companies grew and changed. The same obstacles all entrepreneurs face.

TREPS
/treps/ n: A Millennial name for a modern day entrepreneur. Individual dedicated and focused on growing personally and professionally. Treps take risks and pursue their dreams. Treps refers to people who start a business with a lot of passion and little (or no) money.

NEST
/nest/ n: A place for Treps to incubate, grow and hatch their invention, idea and/or business.

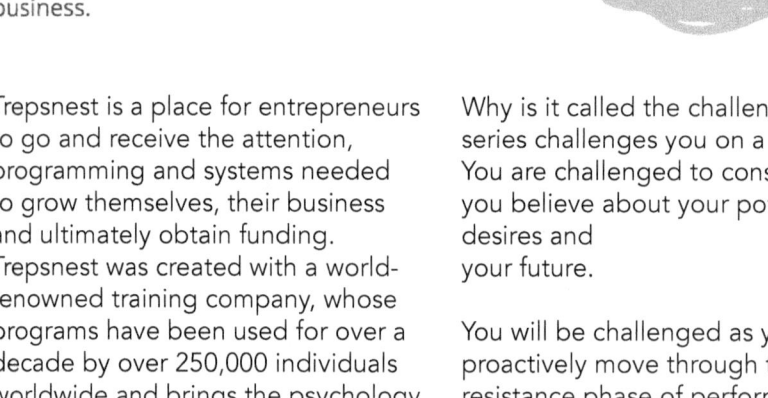

Trepsnest is a place for entrepreneurs to go and receive the attention, programming and systems needed to grow themselves, their business and ultimately obtain funding. Trepsnest was created with a world-renowned training company, whose programs have been used for over a decade by over 250,000 individuals worldwide and brings the psychology and training used with Forbes 500 companies and Forbes 400 Richest People in America. Ultimately, we created Trepsnest to train successful entrepreneurs.

As human beings we are creatures of habit. We tend to do the same things over and over; we like to be in our comfort zones avoiding the uncertainty that comes with change. Studies show that it takes 21-40 days to break or build a habit.

Why is it called the challenge? This series challenges you on a few levels. You are challenged to consider what you believe about your potential, your desires and your future.

You will be challenged as you proactively move through the resistance phase of performance, uncovering barriers and gaps between your current habits and your desired results.

The 45-day proven process supports you in taking small daily actions toward who you want to be and where you want to go. If you commit and follow through, for 45 days, you will build new habits that support you in every area of your life.

4 PROGRAMS, 1 GOAL

1. 365 DAILY FOCUS
Daily Bite Size Task (Habit)
This complimentary program is focused on providing bite size tasks for the entrepreneur to create successful habits.

2. TREP TRAINING
Habit Formation & Self Guided
One Month training program focused on building the habits necessary to be successful as an entrepreneur.

3. CERTIFIED TREP
Identity (Mindset) Formation & Advisor Guided
Our 45 day program certifies entrepreneurs in areas like: Business Strategy, Business Knowledge, Business Development & Mindset.

4. TREP MASTERY
Identity (Behavior) Formation & Advisor Guided
Once the entrepreneur transform their mindset & behavior patterns, Trep Builder provides guidance & support to maintain a winning edge

The program was intended to provide support and guidance for an entrepreneur at any stage. As they continue to grow and mature in their business, they will begin to experience new issues and be required to continually grow and expand their mindset and behavior patterns if they choose to continue to be successful.

ACCOUNTABILITY
On-Time Point System.
Completion Point System.
Daily reminder emails.

FLEXIBILITY
Viewed from any computing device with Internet access, 24 hour access to complete your daily entries

ADVISOR
Weekly team call with an Advisor supporting and guiding you in the program. Email advisor right from the program.

VIDEOS

Theme Videos with Rod Hairston every week - creator of the 45-Day Challenge Series and author of the book, *Are You Up For The Challenge? Starting Now Not Some Day* (available on Amazon Paper or Kindle)

TEAMS

Friendly competition between other teams. Teams support each other through growth. Chat and connect with members and advisor.

SOCIAL

Chat and connect with members and advisor. Do you accept the challenge? Sign up today and see how your business and life will be impacted.

(trepsnest.com/pr/programs/entrepreneur.asp#enroll)

TREPS LEGAL

Every Entrepreneur wants to protect their idea, startup, and business, and Treps Legal offers a unique blend of legal and business expertise.

Treps Legal was formed with entrepreneurs as the focus in mind, and also because finding an entrepreneurial attorney is key to building the foundation all Treps need when starting out and when transitioning.

The difference is in the expertise, the understanding what is needed and the solutions offered. Whether it's a General Counsel Program or flat fee to help the beginning entrepreneur, Treps Legal addresses an Entrepreneur's legal and
business needs no matter where they are on their journey.

Treps Legal offers...*(see next page)*

TRUSTED LEGAL ADVISORS

Commitment to long term success, the team works to assess and address your initial and on-going legal needs. This advisory approach includes our proprietary on-line assessment to determine your legal needs.

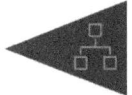

UNIQUE DELIVERY MODEL FOR LEGAL SERVICES

We've created a unique delivery model, the 'General Counsel Platform.' This retainer model consists of a unique blend of customized legal solutions delivered on a monthly basis over a period of six months or one year for an affordable fixed monthly rate. It allows businesses to plan, budget, and manage all of their legal issues. Other offerings include start-up and pre-revenue legal solutions on a per-job or flat fee basis.

CUSTOMIZED LEGAL SOLUTIONS

All of our legal solutions are customized to address the specific and changing needs of new, emerging businesses and includes assessing the nature of our clients business, their organizational strengths and weaknesses, all potential risks and liabilities and their personal and organizational goals to determine the specific legal solutions for their business. This process enables us to get it right the first time and to deliver a combination of legal solutions that address their short and long-term goals.

BUSINESS & LEGAL EXPERTISE & VERSATILE STAFF

Our attorneys are both subject matter experts in their area of the law and are seasoned entrepreneurs. We feel that knowing the law is not enough…it's also necessary to understand the many financial, organizational and cultural challenges our clients face. This holistic approach to law and business enables us to provide richer recommendations and solutions that address their critical legal and business issues.

AFFORDABLE FLAT FEE PROJECTS

Our fee arrangements are scaled and priced to accommodate the needs of each client – we don't bill for phone calls and other miscellaneous tasks. This philosophy enables our clients to get the legal solutions they truly need and allows us to build long term strategic relationships.

TREPS FUNDING

When growth starts to happen, money is one way to ensure it continues. But with so many sources to go to, where does an entrepreneur start? With Treps Funding! Treps Funding has expertise in many forms and connections that will make it easier for an entrepreneur to focus on what's most important: running & growing the business.

Treps Funding's experts have experience in Crowdfunding, SEC 'Regulation D,' and dealing with Venture Capitalists (VC) and Angel Investors.

They know what is needed to be compliant with state and federal regulations as well as know how to approach and pitch VCs and Angel Investors.

CROWDFUNDING is the process of asking the general public for contributions to fund a new project. Treps Funding's team has an extensive background in Crowdfunding, and Michael S. Melfi has authored the book *The Simple Secrets of Crowdfunding* that is an industry handbook on the ins and outs of Crowdfunding.

REGULATION D Changes to the SEC 'Regulation D' have made it easier for companies to increase the number of investors a company can solicit and sell securities to without undergoing the cost of registering with the SEC. Our team has a strong background in traditional capital raising and private placements as well as crowdfunding.

VENTURE CAPITALISTS (VC) AND ANGEL INVESTORS are wealthy individuals who provide seed money for businesses in exchange for convertible debt or ownership equity. Treps Funding's network of local and national VC firms and Angel Investors can get you in front of these affluent individuals once you are ready.

Our Treps Nest team understands the complexity of an Entrepreneurial organization that is growing, because we are Entrepreneurs. We know and understand the struggles and the rewards. Because of that, we offer a unique approach in all our services and programs. We've taken our two decades of working with thousands of Entrepreneurs with their needs and formed programs to help Entrepreneurs navigate the business, the law to ensure they are in compliance, and to develop the mindset and habits critical for success.

Our team is balanced with seasoned professionals and experts who know and understand the impact of every move, the ramifications surrounding Entrepreneurs and the intricacies of running a business day-to-day. We provide creative solutions that we know will benefit your business. To see where you are in the process, take our survey (http://bit.ly/1RPKZ1o) to see if you are ready to enroll in Treps Nest.

ENTREPRENEURIAL SURVEY

What is your blueprint for success? After reading this book and working on your idea, business and dream, you should have an idea of your vision of success. Sometimes, getting the vision to become a reality can be challenging.

That's where our Entrepreneurial Blueprint For Success survey comes in. By answering a set of brief questions, you will assess where you are at and where you want to go. We can customize a plan just for you and your business and where you are in the process to get to the next level.

If your needs are legal, funding or personal & professional growth, our team of experts in Treps Legal, Treps Nest and Treps Funding are here to help you draft your blueprint for success. Make time to focus on your next level by taking the survey now: (http://bit.ly/1MbQelY)

WHAT PEOPLE ARE SAYING ABOUT TREPS NEST

"The program delivered way more impact than I ever imagined. All of the big decisions we make in life are preceded by lots of little choices we make every day, but few of us recognize that. I completed the program with a greater awareness of where I want to go, what I want to have in my life, and most importantly, who I want to be. If you want these things, I strongly recommend you take the program."

-Maureen K., Entrepreneur

"Overall, it was an awesome process. Daily I bump into things that bring up pieces of the process - sometimes they are gentle reminders, sometimes a two-by-four upside my head - whatever I happen to need at the time."

-Marcus L.

"Thanks so much for the great work you and your team do!!! You are changing the world - one person at a time."

-Richard B.

THE SIMPLE SECRETS OF INTELLECTUAL PROPERTY is an overview of the different types of Intellectual Property and how they are protected in the United States, and globally. The goal of the book is to offer the reader some insight when determining if they have Intellectual Property and guidance when deciding how to protect their Intellectual Property. This book is written in simple language to help the reader understand their rights and the rights of others as it relates to Intellectual Property. However, the book should not be used in place of sound legal advice from a licensed attorney, but look on as a guide before contacting an attorney. an overview of the different types of Intellectual Property and how they are protected in the United States, and globally. The goal of the book is to offer the reader some insight when determining if they have Intellectual Property and guidance when deciding how to protect their Intellectual Property. This book is written in simple language to help the reader understand their rights and the rights of others as it relates to Intellectual Property. However, the book should not be used in place of sound legal advice from a licensed attorney, but look on as a guide before contacting an attorney.

In *THE SIMPLE SECRETS OF BEING AN ENTREPRENEUR*, Michael S. Melfi shares all the knowledge and wisdom gained from billionaire mentors and millionaire clients.

Michael has been fortunate enough to work with many successful (and not so successful - remember 90% of businesses are out of business in 5 years) entrepreneurs and business people over the years. In these experiences, he gained an inside look into what it takes to not only make it in business but thrive!

The book covers:
• Uncovering the secret characteristics that successful
  entrepreneurs all have in common?
• How to create focus to have the characteristics of
  successful entrepreneurs.
• Your Entrepreneurial Type (did you know there was such a thing?)
• Tips and tricks of creating an entrepreneurial culture

THE SIMPLE SECRETS OF SOCIAL MEDIA is the ultimate play book for using Social Media in business. In the book written by Michael Melfi, you will get a play by play on how to utilize Social Media strategies for your company. It is essentially a breakdown of how to execute a digital solution for your online problems and needs. The digital solution provides various marketing and promotional initiatives, very similar to a traditional marketing campaign. Over the pages of this book, the reader will achieve some amazing results utilizing various Social Media platforms and digital strategies. By the end of this book the reader will be able to achieve three goals: COMMUNITY DEVELOPMENT, TRUSTED & AUTHENTIC COMMUNICATION, and ACTION.

GLOSSARY

REFERENCE

Accredited Investor
(1) An individual with a net worth, or joint net worth with the person's spouse, that exceeds $1 million at the time of the purchase, excluding the value of the primary residence of such person
or
(2) An individual with income exceeding $200,000 in each of the two most recent years or joint income with a spouse exceeding $300,000 for those years and a reasonable expectation of the same income level in the current year.
SOURCE: *http://www.sec.gov/answers/accred.htm*

Barker
Someone who promotes a project frequently across various online venues. They may write about it on their blog, post links via Twitter or Facebook, and otherwise attract more traffic. Some projects have perks for linkbacks or other promotional activities. A barker may or may not also be a patron; promotion is an excellent way to support a project for people who don't have much money.

Business Plan
A written document describing the nature of the business, the sales and marketing strategy, and the financial background, and containing a projected profit and loss statement.
SOURCE: *http://www.entrepreneur.com/encyclopedia/term/82322.html#*

Capital
(1) Wealth in the form of money or property, used or accumulated in a business by a person, partnership, or corporation
or
(2) Material wealth used or available for use in the production of more wealth.
SOURCE: *http://www.thefreedictionary.com/capital*

Crowdfund Investor Investment Limitations

Investors that make less than $100,000 annually can invest the greater of $2,000 or 5% of their annual income.

Investors whose annual income or net worth is greater than or equal to $100,000 can invest 10% of their annual income.

Crowdfunding Platform (CFP)

Crowdfunding platforms are Internet websites that provide a way for a large number of people (the crowd) to provide money in small increments (the funds) in support of a person, project or entity.
SOURCE: *http://www.quora.com/How-would-you-define-crowdfunding-or-crowdfunding-platforms*

Congress

The national legislative body of the U.S., consisting of the Senate, or upper house, and the House of Representatives, or lower house, as a continuous institution.
SOURCE: *http://dictionary.reference.com/browse/congress*

Crowdcheck

Crowdfunding due diligence company that helps entrepreneurs in crowdfunding or 506(c) offerings make proper disclosure and establish their legitimacy, helping investors avoid fraud.
SOURCE: *https://twitter.com/CrowdCheck*

Crowdfunding

The use of small amounts of capital from a large number of individuals to finance a new business venture.
And/or
A method of raising capital in small amounts from a large group of people using the Internet and social media, where individuals are asked to make micro investments to ventures they believe in.
SOURCE: *http://www.techopedia.com/definition/27815/crowdfunding*
SOURCE:*http://www.investopedia.com/terms/c/crowdfunding.asp#axzz2Lvbz4Ckq*

Development Stage

A company that is in a preliminary or early state of its corporate life. A development stage company is characterized by its focus on early-stage business activities, such as research and development, market research or construction of manufacturing facilities. Development stage companies are

generally underfunded and likely to be interested in different sources of capital.
SOURCE: *http://www.investopedia.com/terms/d/developmentstage.asp#axzz2Lvbz4Ckq*

Diversification

A risk management technique that mixes a wide variety of investments within a portfolio. The rationale behind this technique contends that a portfolio of different kinds of investments will, on average, yield higher returns and pose a lower risk than any individual investment found within the portfolio.
SOURCE: *http://www.investopedia.com/terms/d/diversification.asp#axzz2Lvbz4Ckq*

Due Diligence

Research and analysis of a company or organization done in preparation for a business transaction (as a corporate merger or purchase of securities).
SOURCE: *http://www.merriam-webster.com/dictionary/due%20diligence*

Equity

(1) A stock or any other security representing an ownership interest.

(2) On a company's balance sheet, the amount of the funds contributed by the owners (the stockholders) plus the retained earnings (or losses). Also referred to as "shareholders' equity."
SOURCE: *http://www.investopedia.com/terms/e/equity.asp*

Equity Based Crowdfunding

Financial contributions from online investors to fund for-profit businesses, initiatives or enterprises.

An approach to raising capital for new projects and businesses by soliciting contributions from a large number of stakeholders following the model of investment in exchange for equity, profit or revenue sharing.
SOURCE: *http://www.crowdsourcing.org/community/crowdfunding/7*

Equity Based Crowdfunding Platform

Also known as a "funding portal," as defined by the JOBS Act.
Any person acting as an intermediary in a transaction involving the offer or sale of securities for the account of others, solely pursuant to section 4(6) of the Securities Act of 1933, that does not—
(A) offer investment advice or recommendations;
(B) solicit purchases, sales, or offers to buy the securities offered or displayed on its website or portal;
(C) compensate employees, agents, or other persons for such solicitation or

based on the sale of securities displayed or referenced on its website or portal; **(D)** hold, manage, possess, or otherwise handle investor funds or securities; or **(E)** engage in such other activities as the Commission, by rule, determines appropriate.

SOURCE: *http://www.sec.gov/divisions/marketreg/tmjobsact-crowdfundingintermediariesfaq.htm*

Fans

Individuals who promote the project on social media channels, etc. May not be a funder or barker necessarily.

Founders

Individuals who have ideas, companies, and/or projects that they have founded.

Funders

Individuals who give money to a crowdfunding project. In the case of equity-based crowdfunding, may also be "Investors" and in the case of donation-based crowdfunding, may also be called "Donators."

General Solicitation

Seeking interest from the public at large for an offering either through advertising or some type of mass communication. For a private placement to qualify for the exemption from registration under Regulation D, no general solicitation may take place until the SEC releases regulations under Title II of the JOBS Act.

SOURCE: *http://reversemerger.dealflowmedia.com/rm_glossary.cfm*

JOBS Act

The JOBS Act (Jumpstart Our Business Startups Act) is legislation that eases regulatory restrictions for new businesses to make it easier for startups to get established. The intention of the Act is to encourage more business startups, foster their success, and as a result, create more jobs and stimulate the economy. As stated in the bill, which passed as H.R. 3606, the purpose is "to increase American job creation and economic growth by improving access to the public capital markets for emerging growth companies."

SOURCE: *http://whatis.techtarget.com/definition/JOBS-Act-Jumpstart-Our-Business-Startups-Act*

Market Share

The specific percentage of total industry sales of a particular product achieved by a single company in a given period of time.

SOURCE: *http://dictionary.reference.com/browse/market+share*

Pitch

A short, succinct speech about a business that defines the item, demonstrates its value, and usually has a sales-related call to action at the end. Also called "Sales Pitch" or "Elevator Pitch."

Private Company

A company whose shares are not traded on the open market.

SOURCE: *http://www.investorwords.com/3851/private_company.html*

Regulation D ("Reg D")

A Securities and Exchange Commission (SEC) regulation governing private placement exemptions. Reg D allows usually smaller companies to raise capital through the sale of equity or debt securities without having to register their securities with the SEC.

SOURCE: *http://www.investopedia.com/terms/r/regulationd.asp#axzz2M2T7Buk8*

Return on Investment

The amount of profit, before tax and after depreciation, from an investment made, usually expressed as a percentage of the original total cost invested. Also called "ROI."

SOURCE: *http://dictionary.reference.com/browse/return+on+investment*

Securities and Exchange Commission

The primary federal regulatory agency for the securities industry, whose responsibility is to promote full disclosure and to protect investors against fraudulent and manipulative practices in the securities markets. Also called the "SEC."

SOURCE: *http://www.investorwords.com/4417/SEC.html*

Share

A unit of ownership interest in a corporation or financial asset.

SOURCE: *http://www.investopedia.com/terms/s/shares.asp#axzz2M2T7Buk8*

Shareholder

The owner of one or more shares of stock in a corporation. Also called a "stockholder."

SOURCE: *http://legal-dictionary.thefreedictionary.com/shareholder*

Transparency

The extent to which investors have ready access to any required financial information about a company such as price levels, market depth and audited financial reports.

SOURCE: *http://www.investopedia.com/terms/t/transparency.asp#axzz2M2T7Buk8*

Vetting

A thorough and diligent review of a prospective person or project prior to a hiring or investment decision.

SOURCE: *http://www.investopedia.com/terms/v/vetting.asp#axzz2M2T7Buk8*

http://www.earlyshares.com/university/glossary-of-terms

http://zoshpit.com.au/docs/glossary

http://crowdfunding.dreamwidth.org/127729.html

http://crowdfunding.dreamwidth.org/128259.html

APPENDIX I

VIDEO

Producing Your Video: Some Basic Steps

1. Write a script for the story you want to share (see more "Story - Crafting" tips below)

2. Storyboard your video, or create rough sketches for what you want the camera to show during the video, and when.

3. Recruit a friend or professional service to assist with filming, lighting and sound. No matter your level of production, flattering lighting, a clear resolution, and well executed speaking are very important.

4. When going for a take, remember to breathe, take your time and be natural. While you can always have a do-over, we suggest stopping after a few good takes. That's all you need!

5. Be meticulous in your editing. You may only use 20% of what you record. Transitions, sound and color balance are important, but flow from shot to shot is key. It needs to feel intuitive and natural. iMovie works just as well as Final Cut Pro for the functionality required to make a decent campaign video.

6. Gather opinions after the first cut. How does the video feel to them? Does anything stick out? Make sure you are creating the impression that you want.

Crafting Your Video: Diving into the Story

1. Funders admire a project for its efforts more than for its successes.

2. Keep in mind what a good cause/ or good idea means to you as a

founder, may be very different to what's fun/meaningful as a funder.

3. Trying for results is important, but you won't see what the project is actually about until you have a plan. If you haven't completed this step, stop now and draft your business plan.

4. What's the essence of your story? Most economical telling of it? If you know that, you can build out from there.

5. Tell your story. To help you get started, fill in these blanks: It started with ___. Every day, ___. One day ___. Which led to, ___. Until finally ___. Now,_____.

6. Simplify. Focus. Combine events. Hop over detours and setbacks in your project. You'll feel like you're losing valuable stuff but it actually sets you free.

7. What is the purpose/intention behind your project? What if you found out the project did not represent that original purpose? Would you recreate it, look at it differently?

8. Come up with an exit to your project before you figure out how to make money. Seriously. Exits are hard, get yours in your plan.

9. Finish your video storyboard, even if it's not perfect. In an ideal world it's a knockout, but move on. Learn and do better next time.

10. When you're stuck on developing your project video, make a list of what WOULDN'T work. Many times the ideas to get unstuck will become clear.

11. Go back to your video research and pull apart the project videos you like. What did you like about them; you've got to recognize and understand what it is before you can apply them to your video.

12. Putting your video storyboard on paper lets you begin to refine it. Once you have your storyboard, you may realize your story needs clarification, focus or refining; or that it will not have the impact you want.

13. Don't be afraid to discount your first, second and even your fifth draft of your storyboard; stay open to changes and stay engaged with the process.

14. Give your message passion; passive/malleable might seem likable to you as you write, but it's poison to the audience's ear.

15. Why must you share about THIS project? What's the belief burning within you that your project feeds off of, what is your passion behind it? That's the heart of it. Make that the priority.

16. If you were to get this project funded, how would you feel? Honesty lends credibility to unbelievable situations.

17. What are the stakes? Give us reason to root for the project. What happens if the project does not succeed? Stack the odds against.

18. Just because something isn't working in a certain scenario, doesn't mean it won't work in another. Don't hesitate to let something go that's not working for your project, but keep your ideas/files, as it may be useful at a later time.

19. When trying to complete your project video, you have to know yourself: recognize when your best is good enough.

20. Coincidences for a project are fate; failures only make the story better.

21. Exercise: take the building blocks of a videos you dislike. How would you rearrange them into what you DO like?

22. You must personally identify with your project, can't just write "fund me." What would make YOU act that way?

Questions to ask about your video
Key questions with video
- Who are you?
- Why is your background relevant to this project? Why should your target audience (funder) trust you?

What is your project?

- What's so special or unique about it?
- What does it look like?
- How long will it take to complete the project?
- How much funding do you need to complete the project?
- How will you use the money? Be specific.
- What rewards are you offering? Be specific.
- What will you do if you get more money than you are asking for?
- Why is your project worth viewers' hard-earned dollars?
- How will you keep in touch with the community during development, and after the product is released/ service begins, after the campaign ends?
- Be reasonable with your call to action, your financial goals and what you can realistically accomplish.
- Can you deliver on what you promise?

APPENDIX II

PROJECT PREP

Questions to ask about your project

- How good is your idea, really?
- Why is your product or service destined to sell? What value/benefit does it offer?
- How are you different from the competition, or substitutes?
- Can you express your idea simply and get people excited about it?
- Do you have something tangible to show your audience such as a product, graphs, photos of your charity?
- What research do you need to complete to understand your audience? How well do you know your targets?
- Are you confident in your ability to reach out and connect with backers?
- Have you calculated exactly how much money you need to make to realize your ideas?
- Have you considered all financial variables, such as platform processing, reward fulfillment and taxes? Did you include them in your budget?
- What does your budget look like? Is there wiggle room?
- Can you deliver on all of your promises?
- What do the reward tiers look like? Are they incentivizing to all levels of funding?
- What is unique about these rewards? How will they get people talking?
- Are you committed to the time/energy/resources needed to do a successful CF campaign?
- Do you have some social media/business/marketing savvy? Do you have someone on your team with these skills?
- What will you do after the launch? After the campaign?
- How will you cultivate pre- and post-buzz about the project? Are your tactics included in your plan and budget?

- Are you willing to take the risks associate with your project?
- Do you, and a few trusted/credible people, fully believe in your project?
- Who can you turn to for help? (Legal, financial, marketing assistance, advice, spreading the word?)

Questions to ask about other projects
The Product/Service Event:
- Is it interesting to the casual observer?
- Is it compelling enough to fund?
- What makes it unique?
- What value does it offer?
- What audience was it intended for?
- How would you describe the project in 3 words?
- What would be your elevator pitch for this project? Say it.

The Pitch
- How do they introduce the project?
- Was it clear? Was it accurate? Did you understand?
- Who does it speak to?
- Was it compelling? Why or why not?
- How long did it take you to fully understand the project?
- What were the key details described?
- Did they cut to the chase?
- When, if any, was there a call to action?
- Personal vs. project information offered?
- How often is this information updated?
- Did they address all of your questions as a potential funder/investor?

The Video
- Is it interesting or boring?
- Does it seem authentic or forced?
- Was the production quality poor or exceptional?
- Did you find it engaging, entertaining, or repetitive and long winded?
- Did it capture your interest and did you watch the whole thing?
- Were all your questions answered?
- How much of the project were you actually shown?
- Who did you connect to: the people, or the project itself?
- Was there a direct request/call to action?

- Contact information?
- What made you want to keep watching?

The Rewards
- Do they make sense with the scope of the project?
- Are there enough of them at the different pay tiers?
- Is there value exchanged for money? How, why or why not?
- For a longer standing project...which rewards were the most successful/ quintessential?
- Were these fixed at the beginning, or were more announced later?
- Did fans contribute any rewards?
- Did fans contribute any stretch goals?
- Were any rewards specific or exclusive to the promotion itself?

The Funding Goal
- Is it reasonable based on the parameters of the project?
- Why did some projects fail? Were they compelling, realistic, engaging, clear?
- Can any success factors apply to your project?
  - Past/present notoriety of project owners/others involved
  - Existing fanbase
  - Uniqueness of audience and appeal
  - Uniqueness of rewards
  - Size of target: Funding goal set
  - Presentation of project - written, visual, oral.
  - Other factors?
- Were there stretch goals? Which types were the most successful?
- How was the community involved?

Marketing and PR
- Were the ads, marketing, pr activities related to project promotion?
- What channels were efforts focused on?
- Which were the most/least effective tactics?
- What type of media attention did they attract? What types of publications? What other outlets (radio, television, online media, etc.)?
- How did fans/journalists react to various promotions?
- What resonated best, and why?

- What generated the least response, and why?

Task List: 150 Days of Your Campaign
Here is a laundry list of the things you need to have done (in order), and when. While no one item is necessarily "required," we recommend them as incumbent pieces to crowdfunding success.

Pre-Launch (Day 0-59)
- Write a business plan
- Write an executive summary
- Market Research
- Financial Research/Develop a budget
- Strategy/Business Research
- Make a sizzle reel
- Create a logo & brand
- Legal Research
- Research possible CFPs & sign up
- Onboard Early Funders
- Create/Test prototype
- Create Marketing Plan/Strategy
- Determine Rewards
- Systemize your outreach
- Create buzz around your project
- Become partially funded
- Determine desired seed-funders
- Create a campaign video

Launch (Day 60)
- Now's the time!
- Host a fabulous launch party through social media, webinar or in person. Seriously.
- Execute, everything.
- Failure to Launch?
  - Evaluate, everything.
  - What went wrong?
  - Create a game plan to reboot or abort.

Post-Launch (Day 61-150) and Beyond!
- Video Blog updates to funders, fans and fliers.
- Continuously engage; last minute push for funds
- Reach out to targets who showed interest but have yet to donate
- Exit activities:
  - Ship out promised rewards.
  - Thank you and follow up email to all who donated
  - Continued updates to the project

Example Financial Worksheet							
	Funding Amount	Estimated Number	Cost per Reward	Shipping per Reward	Funding Revenue	Process Cost	Net
Main Project						$11,000	
Website Expenses						$700	
Other (Video, Creative, etc.)						$300	
TOTAL FIXED COSTS						$12,000	
Pledges & Rewards	Funding Amount	Estimated Number	Cost per Reward	Shipping per Reward	Funding Revenue	Process Cost	Net
Reward 1: Digital Content Emailed to Backer							
Standard	12	250	0	0	3000	0	3000
Bulk Order	12	0	0	0	0	0	0
International	12	0	0	0	0	0	0
Number of Rewards		250					
Reward 2: Small Item by Mail (DVD, T-Shirt, etc.)							
Standard	25	200	5	3	5000	1600	3400
Bulk Order	25	12	4	3	300	84	216
International	35	10	4	7	350	110	240
Number of Rewards		222					
Reward 3: Customized Item + Personalized Service							
Standard	75	100	10	6	7500	1600	5900
Bulk Order	75	10	8	6	750	140	610
International	100	5	8	14	500	110	390
Number of Rewards		115					
Total Pledges					17400		
Platform Fee (5%)					870		
Payment Processing (3-5%)					696		
Total Rewards Costs						3644	
Bottom Line					**You Get**	**Costs**	**Excess**
					15834	15644	190

Expected Results Projection

Description		Value
Retail Price		$80
Number of Sales		1200
% of Sales International		30%
Domestic Shipping Allowance		$10
International Shipping Allowance		$15
Total Expected Project Revenue		96000

APPENDIX III

SOCIAL MEDIA

Sample Twitter and Facebook Posts

Twitter sample:

Thank you JOHN SMITH for your great contribution to my project! Supporters like you will get me to my goal!

(Link to project; use image from project since you can now upload images to Twitter.)

And

We have another supporter of _____ Thank you JOHN SMITH for your support!

(Link to project; use image from project.)

Facebook sample:

Thank you JOHN SMITH for your great contribution to our project, _____. Please let your friends and family know you are a supporter! With your help, we'll reach our goal quickly!

(Link to project; use image from project.)

And

We have another supporter of _____ Thank you JOHN SMITH for your support!

(Link to project; use image from project.)

APPENDIX IV

BUSINESS & INVESTMENT

Top 12 Business Incubators (ranked by Forbes)

1. Y Combinator (Mountain View, CA) *http://ycombinator.com*
2. Massachusetts Biomedical Initiatives (Worcester, MA) *http://massbiomed.org*
3. Houston Technology Center (Houston, TX) *http://houstontech.org*
4. Palo Alto Research Center (Palo Alto, CA) *http://parc.com*
5. The Technology Innovation Center (Evanston, IL)
   http://www.theincubator.com/
6. The ICEHouse (Auckland, New Zealand) *http://www.theicehouse.co.nz*
7. The Research Center at University of Illinois - Urbana Champaign (Champaign, IL) *http://illinois.edu/research/reasearch.html*
8. The Advanced Technology Development Center at the University of Georgia (Atlanta, GA) *http://www.atdc.org/*
9. MGE Innovation Center (Madison, WI) *http://universityresearchpark.org/*
10. The Environmental Business Cluster (San Jose, CA)
    http://www2.cleantechopen.org
11. Seedcamp (National) *http://www.seedcamp.com*
12. DreamIt Ventures (Philadelphia, PA) *http://www.dreamitventures.com*

Angel Investor Groups (ranked by entrepreneur.com)

Ohio TechAngel Funds
Columbus, OH
www.ohiotechangels.com
Number of angels: 282
Who it helps: Supports early-stage Ohio-based information technology, advanced materials, and medical technology companies.

Tech Coast Angels

Los Angeles, CA

www.techcoastangels.com

Number of angels: 263

Who it helps: Provides connections, knowledge, mentoring and operational assistance to early-stage entrepreneurs in the tech, biotech, consumer products, Internet, information technology, life sciences, media, software and environmental markets.

Investors' Circle

San Francisco, CA

www.investorscircle.net

Number of angels: 225

Who it helps: Uses private capital to promote businesses that address social and environmental issues. The group has invested almost $150 million in 225 companies, it says.

Golden Seeds LLC

New York, NY

www.goldenseeds.com

Number of angels: 190

Who it helps: Members invest directly, or through a managed fund, in companies that are founded by or led by women. Sectors include consumer products, technology, software and life sciences.

Related Video: How to Land Angel Funding

North Coast Angel Fund

Cleveland, OH

www.northcoastangelfund.com

Number of angels: 180

Who it helps: Invests in Ohio-based technology startups.

Band of Angels

Menlo Park, CA

www.bandofangels.com

Number of angels: 136

Who it helps: Group of former and current high-tech executives that has invested almost $200 million in early-stage technology companies.

Hyde Park Angel Network
Chicago, IL
www.hydeparkangels.com
Number of angels: 133
Who it helps: Members invest in seed and early stage businesses, primarily located in the Midwest. Industries include: information technology, business services, industrial technology, financial services, consumer or industrial products and healthcare services.

Alliance of Angels
Seattle, WA
www.allianceofangels.com
Number of angels: 100
Who it helps: Early-stage investors in startups based in the Northwest region of the country.

Pasadena Angels
Altadena, CA
www.pasadenaangels.com
Number of angels: 100
Who it helps: Provides up to $750,000 in early-stage and seed financing to startups in southern California.

New York Angels Inc
New York, NY
www.newyorkangels.com
Number of angels: 99
Who it helps: Made up of entrepreneurs, CEOs, venture capitalists and other business leaders, the group invests between $250,000 and $750,000 in early-stage technology companies generally located in the Northeast.

Read more: *http://www.entrepreneur.com/article/220149#ixzz2dr4GdySX*

List of VC Networks and Institutions

1. Accel Partners
Deal Types: Emerging Tech Companies
www.accel.com
2011-2012 Exits: Amobee (acquired by Singapore Telecommunications), Brightcove, Facebook, Groupon, Kosmix (acquired by Walmart), Mu Dynamics

(acquired by Spirent), NextG Networks (acquired by Crown Castle), Trulia
Total Exit Value: $53.938 billion

2. Greylock Partners

Deal Types: Consumer Software Companies
www.greylock.com
2011-2012 Exits: Instagram (acquired by Facebook), Facebook, LinkedIn, Palo Alto Networks, Workday, Zynga
Total Exit Value: $67.217 billion

3. Andreessen Horowitz

Deal Types: Biotechnology Companies
www.a16z.com
2011-2012 Exits: Instagram (acquired by Facebook), Facebook, Nicira Networks (acquired by VMware, Skype (acquired by Microsoft)
Total Exit Value: $60.360 billion

4. Meritech Capital Partners

Deal Types: (Late Stage) Internet, Media and Technology Companies
www.meritechcapital.com
2011-2012 Exits: BlueArc (acquired by Hitachi Data Systems), Facebook, NextG Networks (acquired by Crown Castle), PopCap Games (acquired by Electronic Arts)
Total Exit Value: $52.501 billion

5. Founders Fund

Deal Types: Aerospace and Biomedical Technology Companies
www.foundersfund.com
2011-2012 Exits: Facebook, Yammer (acquired by Microsoft)
Total Exit Value: $50.8 billion

6. Sequoia Capital

Deal Types: Emerging Tech Companies
www.sequoiacap.com
2011-2012 Exits: Amobee (acquired by Singapore Telecommunications), Aster Data Systems (acquired by Teradata), Cafe Press, Clearwell Systems (acquired by Symantec), Cotendo (acquired by Akamai), InfoBlox, Instagram (acquired by Facebook), Jive Software, LinkedIn, LitePoint (acquired by Teradyne),

LogLogic (acquired by TIBCO Software), Loopt (acquired by Green Dot), Palo Alto Networks, Provigent (acquired by Broadcom), ServiceNow
Total Exit Value: $23.793 billion

7. Benchmark Capital
Deal Types: Technology, Social, and Mobile Companies
www.benchmark.com
2011-2012 Exits: Ambarella, Bytemobile (acquired by Citrix Systems), Clicker (acquired by CBS), Cotendo (acquired by Akamai), Demandforce (acquired by Intuit), Digital Fuel (acquired by VMWare), Gaikai (acquired by Sony), HipLogic (acquired by Zynga), Instagram (acquired by Facebook), Mu Dynamics (acquired by Spirent), NorthStar Systems (acquired by SEI), Proofpoint, Riot Games (acquired by Tencent), Servicesource, Terracotta (acquired by Software), Tropos (acquired by ABB), Ubiquiti Networks, Yelp, Zillow, Zipcar
Total Exit Value: $8.432 billion

8. Bessemer Venture Partners
Deal Types: Communications Companies
www.bvp.com
2011-2012 Exits: Endeca (acquired by Oracle), LinkedIn, Millennial Media, Ubiquiti Networks, Yelp
Total Exit Value: $15.665 billion

9. New Enterprise Associates
Deal Types: Information Technology and Biomedical Technology Companies
www.nea.com
2011-2012 Exits: Fusion-io, Groupon, Loopt (acquired by Green Dot), Millennial Media, Nicira Networks (acquired by VMware), RingCube (acquired by Citrix Systems), Workday
Total Exit Value: $7.113 billion